REAGAN
and
GORBACHEV

REAGAN
and
GORBACHEV

Michael Mandelbaum and Strobe Talbott

A Council on Foreign Relations Book

Vintage Books · A Division of Random House · New York

Council on Foreign Relations Books

A Vintage Original, February 1987
First Edition

Copyright © 1987 by Council on Foreign Relations, Inc.

Library of Congress Cataloging Publication Data
Mandelbaum, Michael.
  Reagan and Gorbachev.
  "A Council on Foreign Relations book."
  1. United States—Foreign relations—Soviet Union.
  2. Soviet Union—Foreign relations—United States.
  3. Reagan, Ronald.
  4. Gorbachev, Mikhail Sergeevich, 1931–
  I. Talbott, Strobe. II. Title.
  E183.8.S65M34 1986   327.73047   86-24568
  ISBN 0-394-74721-6

Manufactured in the United States of America
10 9 8 7 6 5 4 3 2 1

Since Reagan and Gorbachev *has two subjects and two authors, it is appropriate that it should have two dedications.*

Michael Mandelbaum dedicates this book to his friend and colleague, Nicholas X. Rizo-poulos, who has done so much to encourage his work.

Strobe Talbott dedicates it to his sons, Devin and Adrian, who know and care a great deal about the world in which they are growing up, and who have already be-gun to make it a better place.

CONTENTS

PREFACE

This book grew out of our participation in a study group on U.S.-Soviet relations sponsored by the Council on Foreign Relations. The group held five meetings in the first half of 1986 that were chaired by Henry Grunwald.* We are grateful to him for conducting the meetings, to Paul Kreisberg for organizing them, to Kay King for serving as rapporteur, and to the members of the group who gave us the benefit of their knowledge and understanding.

We also wish to express our gratitude for the many useful comments we received on a preliminary draft of the book from Seweryn Bialer, Harold Brown, John Campbell, Henry Grunwald, Thane Gustafson, Ed Hewett, William Hyland, Paul Kreisberg, Gail Lapidus, and Helmut Sonnenfeldt. Anne Hebald Mandelbaum edited the entire manuscript with

*This book is a sequel to *The Russians and Reagan*, published by Vintage Books in 1984 and based largely on the proceedings of a 1983 Council study group, also under Mr. Grunwald's chairmanship.

great skill and sensitivity. Brooke Shearer provided additional editorial advice, as well as care and feeding for us during numerous collaborative sessions. Lissa August assisted us in gathering material, checking facts and making sure that paper moved in the right direction, which was ultimately into the skillful hands of David Kellogg of the Council and Anne Freedgood of Vintage Books. Terry Calway, Alice McLoughlin and Sue Roach provided typing assistance. Each of us would like to add a note of thanks to the institutions that employed us while we were writing this book: the Lehrman Institute, its Executive Director Nicholas X. Rizopoulos and President Robert W. Tucker; and *Time* Magazine, its Chief of Correspondents Henry Muller and Managing Editor Jason McManus. After all this help, any deficiencies that remain are entirely our own responsibility.

This book is an interim report about an episode in the history of Soviet-American relations that ended in mid-October 1986 when the two leaders met in Iceland. It deals with an incumbent American Administration. In describing the actions, and attempting to explain the motivations, of officials who are, in many cases, still in office, it necessarily relies on some sources that must remain unattributed. In gathering and interpreting information, we have taken pains to establish, in our minds and as much as possible in what we have written here, a solid basis for our assertions and interpretations, particularly when they contradict public, official explanations of policy.

The reader will note that the inner workings of the American government are recounted in far greater detail than those on the Soviet side. The imbalance is a lamentable but unavoidable consequence of the pervasive secrecy in which the Soviet government conducts its affairs. The account here of bureaucratic divisions and maneuvering over arms control in Washington is not matched by a similar discussion of Soviet policymaking. This should not be taken to imply any belief on our part that ruling circles in the Kremlin and its neighboring ministries were of one mind about how to deal with the United States. We simply do not know. We look forward to the day when one of the Moscow foreign-affairs institutes will sponsor and publish a book that attempts to go behind the scenes of Soviet policy.

M.M. & S.T.

November 7, 1986

REAGAN
and
GORBACHEV

1

THE TWO LEADERS

Ronald Wilson Reagan, the fortieth President of the United States, and Mikhail Sergeyevitch Gorbachev, the eighth supreme leader of the Soviet Union, met face-to-face twice in less than a year. At both meetings—in Geneva in November 1985, and in Reykjavik in October 1986—the two leaders were reenacting a ritual that had come to have a central place in the political affairs of the planet. Both were meetings of the world's two most powerful men. Each leader controlled an arsenal of nuclear explosives powerful enough to incinerate every city, town, village and farm on earth. Each possessed the kind of power that before the twentieth century existed only in myths. What the two of them chose to do could touch the lives of every one of the earth's five billion inhabitants. It was not surprising that, through the offices of the huge press corps in attendance at both meetings, the whole world was watching.

What the world saw were two men from different backgrounds, with different temperaments, and with different, although overlapping personal agendas.

Each wanted to bolster his credentials as a leader at home. Reagan sought to demonstrate to the American public that after a long political career and an entire first term of saying harsh things about the Soviet Union he could meet and negotiate with the Soviet leader. Gorbachev, newly installed in office, wished to show the Soviet elite that he could hold his own with the telegenic and experienced leader of the other superpower. Both wanted to appear to the rest of the world prudent, responsible guardians of their own nuclear stockpiles.

Each was committed to a project that the policies of the other threatened to block. In pursuit of his dream of a world free of nuclear weapons, Reagan had launched an effort to produce a system of defenses against nuclear attack. The Soviets had fiercely criticized the scheme. At Geneva and Reykjavik the President sought at the very least to protect his plan from their objections and at best to convince Gorbachev that it served the interests of *both* countries. Gorbachev was beginning the huge task of revitalizing the Soviet Union. He was trying to get the country moving after almost a decade of stagnation. He needed a breathing spell in the competition with the United States in order to concentrate on problems at home. He wanted civil if not cordial relations with the other superpower, but not at the expense of any vital Soviet interest and not if this meant permitting the United States to have an important military system—like strategic defense—while the Soviet Union did not.

At their first meeting at Geneva the emphasis was on personal contact between the two leaders. With little formal business to do, the two spent most of their time getting to know each other. For almost five of the total of eight hours of meetings they were closeted together with only interpreters present. There were even meetings between their wives. This format suited Reagan. He believed in person-to-person diplomacy. The moment that perhaps best expressed his preference for doing international business took place in the little poolhouse on the estate at which he was staying, on the shores of Lake Geneva. He and Gorbachev sat chatting in front of a roaring fire. Reagan later called the Geneva meeting "the fireside summit."

As they sat by that fire, the President may have been, in his own mind, laying the groundwork for another scene at a future meeting. It was a scene he had anticipated and discussed well before meeting Mikhail Gorbachev. "I often fantasize," he had said, "about taking Soviet leaders in a helicopter and just flying around, just kind of let them choose where we go, so it wouldn't look like a planned tour, and be able to point down and say, 'Yeah, those houses down there. Yeah, that house with a trailer and a boat on it in the driveway. That's a working man in America. Yes, he lives in that house. He has that boat. He drives that car to work.'. . .They could not show me comparable things in their country."* The implication was that the Soviet leaders might have a change of heart about their country and the world, and might change their policies accordingly. To the President's mind personal experience counted for everything, and strong personalities could change the world. The two men meeting at Geneva could, he believed, alter

*Cited in Laurence I. Barrett, *Gambling with History: Ronald Reagan in The White House* (Garden City, N.Y.: Doubleday, 1983), p. 30.

the course of history if they decided to do so. He said as much, at one point remarking to the General Secretary, "Here we are. Between us, we could come up with things that could bring peace for years to come."

Gorbachev's thoughts on this general issue are not on record, but to the extent that he was a good Marxist he believed that it is broad impersonal forces, of which individual leaders are simply the agents, that shape history. Reagan saw the relationship between the two great nuclear powers as the work of strong leaders; a Marxist would consider it the product of forces beyond their control. Both were right. The relationship between the two most powerful countries in the world was formed by the interaction of the personal visions of the leaders with the tides of ideology, economics, technology, and history itself.

THE IMPACT OF PERSONALITIES

In his first private meeting with Gorbachev at Geneva, Reagan remarked that they both had come originally from small towns. The observation was in keeping with his belief in the personal touch; it was designed to break the ice for the political discussions to come.

At first glance the President's attempt to establish common ground may have seemed misplaced: the differences between the two men were more striking than the similarities. Reagan was the oldest serving President; Gorbachev, at fifty-four, was an uncommonly young General Secretary. They had come to their high offices from quite different vocations. Before entering politics Reagan had a successful career as an actor in the most visible of businesses, the motion-picture industry. Gorbachev toiled for most of his working life in the hidden recesses of the Communist Party in a medium-sized province in southern Russia. The American had come to power by the most public of political arts, the gift of communicating a vision of the nation and its future to his countrymen. The Russian had attained supreme power by maneuvering within an oligarchy of patrons and rivals, operating behind the wall of secrecy that shields Soviet politics from the eyes of the world.

And yet, for all their differences, the two did have some things in common, and these similarities were pertinent to the concerns that had brought them together. Each had proved himself a formidable political leader, Reagan in the five years of his presidency, Gorbachev in the nine months that he had been General Secretary. Both, as it happened, were gifted public speakers. Ronald Reagan was the master of the modern media. His skill on television and radio was at the heart of his ability to lead. Mikhail Gorbachev's fluency and forcefulness came as something of a surprise. Until he attained supreme power he had rarely been heard or seen in public, in conformity with the stringent canons of public conduct that Kremlin etiquette imposes. Perhaps in part because he had been trained as a lawyer (although he had never practiced)—almost as unusual a background for a Soviet leader as Hollywood films are for an American president—he emerged, once free of these restraints, as the best speaker the Soviet public had heard in many years. He has been described as the most eloquent member of the upper echelons of the Party since Leon

Trotsky.* Both men were at home in their public roles. They were comfortable with the trappings and the ceremonies of power. This is not unusual for a Western leader, who must make his career in the public eye. It is out of the ordinary for a Soviet official. Gorbachev showed that he could work a crowd, if not quite like an American politician then certainly quite unlike his predecessors as General Secretary during the last two decades.

Here, too, there was symmetry in their political histories. Both benefited from comparisons with the men they succeeded. Reagan's four predecessors had all been forced from office in one way or another. Each was in some sense a failed president. Their failures raised the question of whether the office of the presidency itself had become unmanageable. Reagan's success made clear that it had not. As for Gorbachev, the three General Secretaries immediately before him had left office in the only way that, by custom, the post can be vacated with honor: they died.** Well before their deaths Leonid Brezhnev, Yuri Andropov, and Konstantin Chernenko had ceased to make even the relatively few public appearances that Soviet protocol requires. Moreover, well before the end the three had also ceased to function effectively even behind the closed doors of the Kremlin.

*The comparison is made in Zhores Medevedev, *Gorbachev* (New York: Norton, 1986), p. 43.

**Georgi Malenkov, who led the Party only briefly, and his successor Nikita Khrushchev were forced out of power by their colleagues. All the other top Party leaders, however, from Lenin to Chernenko, have died in office.

Both Reagan and Gorbachev had put their political skills to good use in consolidating power. For all the differences between the two positions, the American presidency and the office of General Secretary of the Communist Party of the Soviet Union have some institutional features in common. Neither is inherently an all-powerful position. The authority of the incumbent depends in large part on his personal skill at balancing the interests and demands of various constituencies and keeping rivals and opponents at bay. During his first years in office Reagan had become the most powerful President in two decades. The returns were not yet in on Gorbachev, but he had made a start in accumulating formidable power.

Neither was beyond challenge. Both faced political difficulties. Reagan was beginning to feel the constraints of the federal budget. Pressure to reduce the large deficit jeopardized his military program, which was a source of leverage on the Soviet Union. As for Gorbachev, although he had attained the position of General Secretary with impressive dispatch, he had not succeeded in placing people loyal to him personally in key positions throughout the Soviet system, as Khrushchev and Brezhnev had done, to ensure that his policies would be carried out.

Each man did, however, enjoy an unusual measure of authority over foreign policy, especially in dealing with the other superpower. Reagan could make an agreement with the Soviet Union without fear of being criticized for being naive about America's great adversary. Gorbachev had managed to put his own team in place to supervise foreign affairs, and there was a feeling among some in the Soviet elite that a respite from the competition with the West would serve Soviet interests, provided it could be secured on acceptable terms.

Reagan and Gorbachev both came to office at a time of difficulties for their countries at home and abroad. In 1980, when Reagan defeated Jimmy Carter, the United States was reeling from the second oil shock in six years and suffering from double-digit inflation, high interest rates, and extensive unemployment. The Shah of Iran had fallen and been replaced by a rabidly anti-American regime, the humiliating captivity of American embassy personnel in Tehran had dragged on for over a year, and the Soviet Union had planted its flag in Africa and invaded Afghanistan. Five years later, when Gorbachev succeeded Chernenko, it was the Soviet Union that was beset with troubles: a stagnant economy, a troubled society, a restive empire in Europe and beleaguered positions in the Third World.

Without the troubles that beset his country, it is possible that neither man would have risen to the top. Before 1980 Ronald Reagan was widely considered too old, and his political views too extreme, for him to be elected President. Mikhail Gorbachev almost surely aroused the opposite concern in the handful of old men with the power to choose the supreme Soviet leader: he was too young and untried. After the death of Yuri Andropov, Gorbachev was passed over in favor of the safe choice, the elderly, enfeebled Konstantin Chernenko. When Chernenko died, the old guard could not afford yet another decrepit leader. The ill health of the top leader had become something of a joke and a symbol of the condition of the Soviet Union itself.

Gorbachev's selection came quickly and he consolidated his position with unusual speed. The pace of events may have had something to do with the challenge from abroad that the Soviet hierarchy evidently felt. In his speech nominating Gorbachev in a closed session of the Politburo, the venerable Foreign Minister Andrei Gromyko was reported to have said, "Some people abroad long to see disagreements within the Soviet leadership. . . .[But] the Politburo's opinion is unanimous. This time (as in the past) we, the Central Committee and the Politburo, will not give satisfaction to our political enemies on this account."

Reagan and Gorbachev each entered office with a strong and explicit mandate to address the urgent problems facing their countries. It is an established custom of American political life for an incoming President, especially when he is succeeding a member of the opposing party, to stress the disarray in which he finds the nation. This Reagan did in 1981. But it is unusual for a Soviet leader to sound this theme. Yet that is what Gorbachev did. He expressed alarm at the Soviet Union's circumstances: "The historic fate of the country and the position of socialism in the modern world," he said, "depend to a large extent on how we manage things from now on."

The remedies that Reagan and Gorbachev prescribed also had something in common. In domestic affairs each was devoted to the bedrock precepts of his political and economic system. Each believed that the way to reinvigorate his country was to return to traditional principles and practices.

Ronald Reagan was an enthusiastic partisan of the free market and of private enterprise. His formula for economic success was simple: get the government out of the way. He proposed to trim regulations, lower taxes, and let the magic of the market and the drive and ingenuity of individual entrepreneurs do the rest. He was the most unabashed champion of the principles of capitalism to be President since Calvin Coolidge. He took pride in that distinction, hanging a portrait of Coolidge in the White House.

Gorbachev was an orthodox Leninist in his politics, dedicated to the monopoly of power by the Communist Party and opposed to permitting other centers of authority or any spontaneous public conduct; and a latter-day Stalinist in his economics, entirely comfortable with state ownership and with central planning and management of all the farms, factories and services in his country. While Reagan wanted to weaken the grip of the state, Gorbachev proposed to tighten it. His prescription for prosperity involved more discipline, better leadership, and—the great hope of Soviet leaders since Lenin's time—technology. There was talk of encouraging more initiative in the economy. The boundaries of officially permitted discussion in Moscow widened somewhat. But Gorbachev also cracked down on drunkenness, absenteeism, and corruption. And more political freedom certainly had no place in his scheme of things. He was critical of some of the policies of his predecessors and spoke frequently of change; but the changes he envisioned would not alter the basic features of the Soviet economic or political systems.

For the troubles they faced abroad, the two leaders also adopted similar approaches. Neither had had significant exposure to foreign affairs earlier in his political career. Neither had had international responsibilities. Both were strong nationalists and believed that their countries were entitled to leading roles in the world. Neither believed in retreating from positions already held. And, to put it mildly, neither was well disposed toward the designs and ambitions of the other.

There was a marked difference of style between the two men. Reagan's patriotism was sentimental and romantic. He was fond of invoking the Puritan John Winthrop's vision of America as a "city on the hill," a shining example to the world. But in Reagan's view, the nation was not to serve merely as a passive example; it was to be assertively engaged with other countries, spreading the blessings of liberty. By contrast, Gorbachev's style was brisk and hortatory. He initially seemed to be a manager, not a visionary. Yet, just as Reagan was committed to an activist American foreign policy, so Gorbachev had great ambitions for the Soviet Union and its influence around the world. He might pay lip service to the goal of the triumph of the international working class, but Soviet foreign policy had long since come to be driven by the aims of great-Russian nationalism, which had merged with the expansive ambitions of Communist dogma. These ambitions Gorbachev fully embraced. In this way, too, he began his tenure as an orthodox Soviet leader.

Although each man was a relatively strong leader, neither was an entirely free agent. The two were the products, and the representatives, of radically different societies and political systems, which constrained them both. The one was an open republic, founded by great democrats like Franklin, Washington and Jefferson. It was the hub of financial, commercial and

13

cultural networks that stretched around the world. The other was a closed society and political system, still largely shut off from the rest of the world, the creation of a handful of conspiratorial intellectuals led by Lenin, and later of the tyrant Joseph Stalin. The very ideas of independent culture and private commerce were heretical, and the organizing political principle was the control of the many by the self-appointed few.

Small-town boys they may once have been in distant, simpler days, but in the late fall of 1985 Ronald Reagan and Mikhail Gorbachev confronted each other across a wide chasm of interest, ideology, and culture, in fulfillment of Tocqueville's often cited prophecy of one hundred and fifty years before: "The Anglo-American relies upon personal interest to accomplish his ends and gives free scope to the unguided exertions and common sense of the citizens; the Russian centers all the authority of society in a single arm: the principal instrument of the former is freedom, of the latter servitude. Their starting point is different and their courses are not the same; yet each of them seems to be marked out by the will of heaven to sway the destinies of half the globe."

The deep differences between the two societies and their political systems, and the conflicting aspirations to which these gave rise, made coexistence difficult, yet nuclear weapons made it unavoidable. The assertiveness of the two leaders compounded the dilemma. What each wanted the other rejected. For five years Reagan had been trying to cast the relationship in a way that was wholly unacceptable to the Soviet leaders, while Gorbachev's goal—a revitalized, resurgent Soviet Union—was anathema to Reagan.

Their presence at Geneva in November 1985 and at Reykjavik 11 months later signified their mutual recognition that a measure of civility and some form of high-level communication were necessary in Soviet-American relations. Each side had come a long way on this score. Their governments had spent much of the previous four years denouncing each other in terms so harsh that diplomatic engagement, not to mention accommodation, had seemed out of the question. Reagan and Gorbachev modulated the war of words and created an atmosphere in which new initiatives were possible.

It was one thing to recognize the need for a new basis for Soviet-American relations, however, and quite another to establish it. But if Reagan and Gorbachev were not entirely free agents, neither were their hands completely tied. Their seemingly strong positions at home meant that each could, if he chose to do so, commit his country to a particular approach, to a set of guidelines, and to specific agreements. Together they could shape the course of Soviet-American relations. For this there was ample historical precedent.

THE BURDEN OF HISTORY

Chance and circumstance had brought other American Presidents and Soviet Party leaders together before on the stage of history. Their policies defined particular phases of the relationship between the two countries. Those policies, in turn, were fusions of grand, impersonal historical forces and extremely personal visions and initiatives. The achievements and failures of this series of geopolitical odd couples made up the historical legacy that Reagan and Gorbachev brought with them to Geneva.

Woodrow Wilson and Vladimir Lenin were the first of these pairs. The two never met but they became rivals for what would later be called the "hearts and minds" of the world. World War I brought them to positions of international prestige—Lenin through the Russian Revolution that the war triggered, Wilson through America's entry into that war, both in the momentous year 1917. Each was a prophet of a new order in Europe and the world, to be built on the ruins of the old one that four years of bitter fighting had destroyed. Their visions were radically different. Wilson foresaw a world of independent nation-states taking the place of the old multinational empires ruled by the dynastic families that had dominated the European continent for centuries. All the free nations of Wilson's new world would belong to an international organization, the League of Nations, that would resolve disputes and keep the peace. Lenin was the apostle of Communist revolutions that would bring to power workers (or their self-appointed spokesmen, like Lenin himself). They would destroy the class rule of capitalism that had oppressed the laboring people of the world; its inexorable drive for economic expansion had supposedly climaxed in the war itself. The choice between these two visions continued to be relevant long after the original visionaries were gone.

Neither vision came to pass. Instead, the leader of Germany seized the center stage of international politics and proceeded to try, with grotesque brutality and alarming success, to impose his own plan for the future on the peoples of Europe. Adolf Hitler's rampage forged a partnership between Franklin D. Roosevelt, who had been Woodrow Wilson's Assistant Secretary of the Navy, and Joseph Stalin, who had been Lenin's Commissar for Nationalities. They corresponded sporadically and did actually meet twice, in Tehran in 1944 and in Yalta, on the Black Sea, in early 1945. By then Hitler was all but beaten, and the task of the two leaders and British Prime Minister Winston Churchill was to plan for the postwar world. The wartime partnership was the apogee of Soviet-American cooperation. It was a time when the public image that each country had of the other was most favorable.

The postwar dissolution of the partnership involved misunderstanding, disappointment, and at least on the American side a sense of betrayal. The Americans had hoped for the kind of world that Wilson had foreseen. Stalin had quite different ideas for the part of Europe that his forces occupied. When American illusions about the possibility of cordial ties dissolved, what persisted were hard facts on the ground. The armies that Roosevelt and Stalin had commanded met in the center of Europe, where they remain today.

Roosevelt's successor, Harry Truman, presided over the atomic raids on Japan that helped to end World War II, the failure of the Baruch Plan, the first proposal for nuclear disarmament, and the beginning of the political conflict between the two great wartime allies that came to be known as the Cold War. Dwight Eisenhower, who assumed the presidency next, tried, with limited success, to reach some kind of accommodation with the Soviets. The most dangerous moment in the seven decades of Soviet-American relations—the Cuban missile crisis of October, 1962—came during the presidency of Eisenhower's successor, John Kennedy. It was a moment when war seemed imminent. The prospect was terrifying because it could have been nuclear war. The missile crisis brought home in vivid fashion to Kennedy and Nikita Khrushchev, the Soviet leader at the time, the special responsibility that they bore in the nuclear age. Their relations during those two weeks in October were marked by unparalleled urgency. In the aftermath they tried to build a political relationship that could prevent such dangers.

They established a "hot line" to communicate directly and swiftly in case of emergency. Kennedy approved the first American grain sales to the Soviet Union. The two concluded an agreement prohibiting experimental nuclear explosions in the atmosphere, in space, and under water.* It was a modest measure, whose principal effect was to protect the environment from radioactive fallout rather than to slow the arms race; but it was significant as the first formal arms control agreement of the nuclear age.

It is unlikely that either Ronald Reagan or Mikhail Gorbachev was familiar in great detail with the course of Soviet-American relations in the twentieth century. Neither was noted for his interest in history. Reagan had been a student of economics at Eureka College in Illinois fifty years before. He had lived through many of the important events in the rivalry between the two great powers but had never displayed any particular interest in what historians made of them. After studying law at Moscow State

*It was a "Limited" Test Ban Treaty because it permitted testing underground that continues to the present day.

University in the early 1950s Gorbachev had taken a degree by correspondence in agronomy. Undoubtedly intelligent, he would have had to be uncommonly, perhaps recklessly curious to try to piece together an accurate history of the foreign policy of his own country, including its relations with the United States. Full and accurate accounts of the past are not a Soviet specialty. The only version of history permitted is the official version, which is subject to change according to the wishes of the officials of the moment. According to a Russian saying of the Soviet period, "Nothing is harder to predict than the past." An ambitious politician would not be inclined to attempt to understand or even to become closely acquainted with what had happened since 1917.

However, Reagan and Gorbachev did not need to know the history of Soviet-American relations in any detail to be familiar with its most important legacies. Neither needed to be told of the ideological rivalry that Wilson and Lenin had begun, or be reminded of the division of Europe that was the legacy of the policies of Roosevelt and Stalin, or be briefed on the dangers of the nuclear age that had been so vivid for Kennedy and Khrushchev. These were the gravitational forces of international politics, to which Reagan, Gorbachev, and all other world leaders adjusted their policies, often without even thinking. The President and the General Secretary no more needed to know the precise origins of the basic facts of international life than they had to know the origins of the words that they spoke in order to use them properly.

Still, they were very familiar indeed with the achievement of a more recent pair of American and

Soviet leaders, Richard Nixon and Leonid Brezhnev. Reagan and Gorbachev were already significant political figures when Nixon and Brezhnev held their countries' highest political offices. Reagan was governor of California and a former candidate for the presidency—a rival of Nixon's in 1968, in fact—who no doubt had his eye on running again. Gorbachev became First Secretary in Stavropol, an important position, in 1970 and for the last three years of Brezhnev's rule was his colleague in the Politburo in Moscow as Party Secretary for agriculture.

The two leaders were familiar with what Nixon and Brezhnev had done for another reason. While the legacies of Wilson and Lenin, of Roosevelt and Stalin, and of Kennedy and Khrushchev established the basic conditions of the Soviet-American relationship, which Reagan and Gorbachev had to accept, the legacy of Nixon and Brezhnev—détente and its fate—set the agenda for the next stage of the relationship, which the two current leaders had to address.

Nixon and Brezhnev had expanded upon the tentative, small-scale rapprochement that Kennedy and Khrushchev had begun ten years earlier in the aftermath of the missile crisis.*

Moving beyond the hot line, they arranged full-scale summit meetings, which were supposed to take place annually at sites alternating between the two

*The détente of the 1970s was not purely the personal creation of the American President and the Soviet General Secretary. A number of developments made it possible: détente in Europe, especially in Germany; the rapprochement between the United States and the People's Republic of China; the achievement by the Soviet Union of a position of rough nuclear parity with the United States; and the effects of the American war in Vietnam.

countries. Three were held before Nixon resigned the presidency, and his successor, Gerald Ford, met with Brezhnev at Vladivostok in 1974. (Jimmy Carter subsequently met Brezhnev in 1979 in Vienna and signed a major arms treaty.) Building on the first grain sales of the 1960s, Nixon and Brezhnev planned a much more extensive economic partnership, with trade on a broad front and a series of scientific and cultural exchanges that together would form a "web of interdependence" in which both countries would be enmeshed. They also negotiated, and in 1972 signed, a geopolitical code of conduct for the two countries to observe, known as the Statement of Basic Principles, and agreed the next year to a set of norms designed to prevent nuclear war.

The arms control agreements that Nixon and Brezhnev reached were far more sweeping than the initial test ban treaty of 1963. In 1972 they signed a treaty restricting antiballistic missile systems and an interim accord setting limits, although permissive ones, on offensive weapons on both sides. They started a process of negotiation on strategic weapons that continued more or less uninterrupted for more than a decade, becoming a regular feature of East-West relations.

In the wake of the missile crisis, Kennedy and Khrushchev had expressed the hope that they could work out a new relationship between their two countries. Nixon and Brezhnev announced that they had established one and that in the 1970s Soviet-American relations had entered a new, more cordial era.

They were wrong. The 1972 summit and the agreements and declarations that it produced did not inaugurate a period of cooperation and harmony between the two great nuclear powers. The contentious elements in the relationship came to the surface; by the end of the 1970s they dominated it. Opposition to what Nixon was trying to accomplish appeared in the United States soon after the policy of détente had begun. Whether there was opposition to Brezhnev's version of détente in the upper ranks of Soviet officials is impossible to say with any certainty. None was publicly expressed, although there were hints of opposition within the leadership; the dismissal from the Politburo of the Ukrainian Party leader Pyotr Shelest in 1972, on the eve of the first Nixon-Brezhnev summit, was rumored to be connected to disagreements about foreign policy.

Trade between the superpowers remained at low levels. The two economies were not particularly complementary. Moreover, Nixon's promise to give the Soviet Union "most favored nation" trading status, to put it on an equal footing with America's other trading partners, ran afoul of the demand in Congress that in return the Soviet Union allow uninhibited emigration. The Jackson-Vanik Amendment to that end was designed to free the hundreds of thousands of Jews in the Soviet Union who wished to leave. Ultimately a quarter-million did leave, but the Soviet authorities refused to accept any formal conditions for most-favored-nation status and so never received it.

The 1972 Statement of Principles declared that neither side would seek unilateral advantages over the other. Yet both continued to do just that. Each made gains at the other's expense outside Europe. The Soviet Union helped Egypt and Syria attack America's ally Israel in 1973. Israel won the war, however, and in the diplomatic maneuvering that followed the

United States succeeded in bringing Egypt into the Western camp and excluding the Soviets from the Arab-Israeli negotiations. The Soviets benefited from the final success of the Communist campaigns against the pro-Western governments of Indochina in 1975, campaigns that they had generously supported. They subsequently sponsored the dispatch of Cuban troops to Africa to assist pro-Soviet factions and governments there and sent their own forces into Afghanistan at the end of 1979.

As for the Strategic Arms Limitation Talks (SALT), the two countries pledged to follow the 1972 agreements with further restraints on offensive weaponry. But it took seven years to negotiate the second SALT treaty, and then the United States did not ratify it. Perhaps a strong President firmly committed to détente could have preserved more of it. But the architect of the policy, Richard Nixon, was politically weakened, then destroyed by the Watergate scandal, and neither of his two immediate successors was powerful enough to defend it effectively, especially against the attacks of presidential candidate Ronald Reagan in 1976 and 1980.

While opposition to détente in its broadest sense grew in the United States during the 1970s, the three Administrations of that decade did try to protect what they came to see as its core. They fulfilled the terms of the agreements that had been signed. They negotiated with Moscow for further accords. They treated the Soviet Union with a degree of civility if not warmth. And they took part in occasional, if not regular, summit meetings. Until the end of 1979 and the Soviet invasion of Afghanistan, this core remained more or less intact.

The Soviet side, at least publicly, was more unified and enthusiastic in its commitment to the principles and practices of détente. Moscow persistently expressed interest in preserving the atmosphere and agreements achieved in 1972. No doubt the particular combination of benefits that détente offered—the apparent freedom to expand Soviet influence in the Third World and the constraints on American technological virtuosity in the arms race—had much to do with the official Soviet position.

There was, however, another reason for the Soviets' support for détente. It had a symbolic meaning for them. It formally recognized their status as the international equal of the United States. It meant that their country was one of only two members of the most exclusive club in the world, the club of superpowers, with all the attendant rights and privileges. The Communist Party of the Soviet Union had waged a long, arduous struggle to reach the pinnacle of world power. Leonid Brezhnev and his colleagues could remember when their country was not powerful at all—indeed when it was chaotic internally and acutely vulnerable to foreign enemies. They had lived through the famines of the 1930s, Stalin's crushing program of industrialization and his great purges. They had seen Hitler's armies reach the gates of Moscow and Leningrad. They had known the early, anxious days of the postwar rivalry with an even more powerful nation than Germany, one that alone possessed the new weapon of unimaginable force, the atomic bomb. Détente meant that they had left all that far behind. It meant that they had pulled themselves up to the same plateau as the North American giant. It meant that the sacrifice and suffering of Soviet history had earned them a position of respect in the world.

This was the great achievement of Brezhnev and his colleagues in the upper echelon of the Soviet political system. Together they formed a distinct political generation, one that had risen early to power in the shadow of Stalin's purges and had retained its grip on that power for four decades. Twice a year throughout the 1970s, on May Day and the anniversary of the October Revolution, the generation's leading lights assembled on top of Lenin's tomb—Brezhnev himself, Aleksei Kosygin, Mikhail Suslov, Andrei Gromyko, Dimitri Ustinov, Andrei Kirelenko, Yuri Andropov and the others—the dour grey veterans, perpetrators, and survivors of much of Soviet history. In many ways their performance in governing the country they surveyed was disappointing. They had not begun to match, let alone surpass, the affluence of the West, as Khrushchev had boasted they would. They had not built Communism in Russia, as a series of party programs had promised. After seven decades of Party rule they could not even provide their own people with what they considered a suitable diet without help from abroad. They had to buy grain from America.

One thing, however, they had unquestionably done: They had drawn even in military terms with the greatest Western power. Their collection of tanks, warships, planes, and above all nuclear-armed ballistic missiles was second to none. With military parity, they thought, would come political equality. The Soviet Union would, like the United States, be present everywhere. It would take a leading role in the world's political business. There would be, in Andrei

Gromyko's words, "no question of any importance which can be decided without the Soviet Union or in opposition to it."

Gorbachev came to office critical of the Brezhnev generation on a number of counts. But there is no sign that he questioned their one great achievement. Quite to the contrary, he clearly regarded it as part of his inheritance, something beyond dispute. There is every indication that he, like the members of the Brezhnev generation, assumed that the Soviet Union should occupy one of the two highest positions in the councils of world power. He, like they, took as a matter of established fact the military and political equality of the Soviet Union with the United States. He believed, as they had, that his country's military achievement and the political consequences that followed from it had become part of the settled international order, that military parity and political equality were natural, desirable, and irreversible.

Reagan, however, did not believe this. He rejected détente and challenged the developments and attitudes that, in the eyes of the Soviet elite, had produced it. His rejection, and those challenges, helped to produce the deterioration of Soviet-American relations that occurred in the first half of the 1980s and also set in motion the events that, paradoxically, brought the two leaders to Geneva in 1985 and to Reykjavik in 1986.

2

THE REAGAN COUNTER-REVOLUTION

The first Reagan Administration marked a twenty-year low in Soviet-American relations. Not since the series of crises over the U-2, Cuba and Berlin in the early 1960s had there been as much tension and recrimination between Washington and Moscow. Not since the presidency of Harry Truman, in the depths of the Cold War, had an entire four-year term elapsed without a meeting between the American President and a top Soviet leader. Later, Reagan and his aides would blame the prolonged hiatus on the infirmity of the Soviet leadership. For virtually the entire Reagan first term and into the second, the Kremlin was doubling as a geriatric ward and funeral parlor. Asked why Reagan had gone four years without talking directly to his Soviet counterpart, American officials would answer that, in effect, there had been no one to talk to.

But it was also true that Reagan and his team came into office believing that there was nothing to talk about; that, as Reagan put it, after a decade of "neglect. . .weakness and self-doubt" the task of American foreign policy was to conduct a unilateral military buildup and go back on the offensive politically. Reagan's first Secretary of State, Alexander Haig, later recalled in his memoirs the view that prevailed in 1981: "At this early stage there was nothing substantial. . .to negotiate until the U.S.S.R. began to demonstrate its willingness to behave like a responsible power."

This view, and the policies that followed from it, departed sharply from the practices of the Administrations of the 1970s. Reagan's predecessors had worked hard to protect détente from domestic political opposition. Reagan was part of that opposition. He saw little in détente that was worth preserving. He had no use for the generally polite rhetoric and the private communications with Moscow that had marked American policy toward the Soviet Union for almost a decade.

In the 1970s, the long-time Soviet Ambassador to Washington, Anatoly Dobrynin, had assumed an important role. He had been the chief intermediary for relaying American arms-control proposals to Moscow and the Kremlin's responses to the White House. Successive American Secretaries of State and Presidents had come to rely on him for a sense of how the Kremlin would react to Washington's policies. Partly because of this critical and sensitive function, Dobrynin enjoyed special privileges. While other ambassadors entered the State Department through the main lobby, Dobrynin's limousine was permitted to pull into the underground garage, where the Ambassador would be whisked by elevator directly and discreetly to the Secretary's office on the seventh floor, unseen by the press and the public. The Reagan Administration was quick to revoke this privilege. The gesture was seen to symbolize the new Administration's resolve to break with the customs of détente, to stop the unjustified deference that the new American leaders felt the Soviet Union had been receiving, and to open a new era in Soviet-American relations that would be more favorable to the United States.

The Soviets responded to these American gestures by coming out swinging. It is sometimes said that there is nobody more offensive than a Russian on the defensive, and the period from 1981 through much of 1984 offered a great deal of supporting evidence for that view.

Initially, the Soviets had hoped that Reagan, a fire-breathing anti-Communist Republican from California, would, like an earlier example of that species, Richard Nixon, be easier to do business with than quixotic liberal Democrats. Jimmy Carter had embraced Leonid Brezhnev and signed the SALT II treaty at their summit meeting in Vienna in 1979, only to react with shock and anger to the invasion of Afghanistan a few months later and to withdraw the treaty from consideration by the U.S. Senate. The Soviets were not sorry to see Carter leave the presidency, and they were cautiously optimistic about Reagan. But once that optimism was dashed, the men in the Kremlin responded with characteristic overkill: their press depicted Reagan as another Hitler.

Thus, early in the first Reagan Administration, the leadership in both Washington and Moscow returned to the pattern of the late 1940s and early 1950s: harsh rhetoric in public and almost no contact in private. For almost a year, each side attempted a policy of ignoring and isolating the other—and, in the process, of isolating itself. The policy of isolation proved untenable for both sides. As Robert W. Tucker later observed of the United States:

> If our experience in recent years conveys one clear lesson, it is that the public will not support a policy that does not hold out the hope of improvement in our relationship with the Soviet Union, and that does not actively seek improvement. In this respect, as in so many others, there has been a marked change since the period of the Cold War.*

But although the American-initiated isolation ended after the first year of the Reagan Administration, there was no full-scale return to the rules and procedures of the 1970s. A series of developments on the international scene and domestically in both countries blocked or derailed efforts toward the kind of engagement that had characterized the 1970s era of détente. The road from the entrance to the State Department parking garage, where Dobrynin's limousine was turned back in 1981, to the Reagan-Gorbachev summit in Geneva more than four years later was long and difficult.

WALKING OUT AND SHOOTING DOWN

It was public pressure from Western Europe that forced a resumption of arms-control talks on intermediate-range weapons in late 1981, and similar pressure from the U.S. Congress led to the re-opening of strategic-arms talks in 1982. But while public opinion

---

*"Toward a New Détente," *New York Times Magazine*, December 9, 1984.

can lead the superpowers to negotiate with each other, it cannot force them to reach agreements unless they are inclined to do so, and the United States and Soviet Union during the first term of the Reagan Administration were definitely not so inclined. Instead, they were locked in a battle of wills over the scheduled deployment of American intermediate-range missiles in Western Europe at the end of 1983. For both sides, the issue was at least as much political as military. In 1977 the Chancellor of West Germany, Helmut Schmidt, had sounded the alarm over a new generation of Soviet missiles targeted on Western Europe, and had wondered aloud whether the size and nature of the American nuclear arsenal in Europe were still sufficient to guarantee that the United States could, and would, come to its allies' defense if they were attacked. The result, at the end of 1979, was a joint decision by the leaders of the NATO countries to deploy in Europe a new generation of American missiles as a counter to the Soviets'—and as a symbol of the U.S. commitment.

Blocking the NATO deployments very nearly became the centerpiece of Soviet foreign policy. By challenging the legitimacy of even a single American missile, the Soviets attacked the validity of the United States' standing as the senior partner of a transatlantic alliance. Conversely, the prime motivation for the United States to proceed with deployment on schedule was to reaffirm its claim to be the protector of Western Europe against its menacing neighbor to the East.

Thus the arms-control talks in Geneva had less to do with the military characteristics of the weapons under negotiation than with the manipulation of political perceptions. Neither side desired compromise; each was committed to an all-or-nothing objective, with virtually no middle ground between them.

As for strategic weapons, the Reagan Administration held to the proposition that the Soviet Union had pulled dangerously ahead in the size and composition of its nuclear forces. In the American view that meant either the Soviet Union would have to build down or the United States would have to build up—or, better yet, both developments should occur—and no lesser outcome could be the basis of a strategic-arms agreement. Since the Soviets accepted neither the American premise nor the American objective, an agreement on this issue was all but impossible. Although negotiation was largely a cosmetic exercise, even Reagan's decision to send negotiators to Geneva aroused alarm among some who had been among his staunchest supporters.*

Reagan was not only the "Great Communicator" but the great delegator as well. Since there was no Soviet leader with whom he could communicate, he tended all the more to leave the conduct of East-West relations to subordinates. High-level contacts consisted mainly of somber delegations to Kremlin funerals led by Vice President George Bush and whatever business Haig's successor as Secretary of State, George Shultz, could do with the redoubtable Andrei Gromyko. Initially, those contacts were very limited

---

*As examples of the rightist opposition, see Norman Podhoretz, "The Neo-Conservative Anguish Over Reagan's Foreign Policy," *The New York Times Magazine*, May 2, 1982, and George Will's columns in Newsweek, January 18, 1982 ("Reagan's Dim Candle") and June 21, 1982 ("Creeping Haigism").

indeed. For Shultz, the encounters were doubly exasperating: Gromyko, then in his last days as Foreign Minister, was unyielding; and some of Shultz's colleagues in the American government, notably Secretary of Defense Caspar Weinberger, were determined that Shultz not give away anything even if the Soviets were forthcoming. "It takes two to tango," was the President's reply to a query about the prospects for improving relations with the Soviets. But during the last days of Leonid Brezhnev and the brief tenures of Yuri Andropov and Konstantin Chernenko, there wasn't even one willing dancer. Soviet-American relations were in the hands of second-echelon officials who, for different reasons, were able to do very little.

Even in those circumstances there were still—in Congress, in the capitals of the European allies, and even within the Executive Branch of the U.S. government—forces pressing toward accommodation. Their principal agent was Shultz. As he gained influence and confidence, he persuaded Reagan to let him try a bit of quiet diplomacy in order to explore the possibility of negotiating several minor agreements and discussions aimed at reducing regional tensions. Shultz had some interest in seeing whether it might be possible to moderate, if not abandon, the strong initial inclination of the Administration to impose a kind of diplomatic boycott on the Soviet Union. He won some leeway to seek points of agreement. But the two sides passed each other going in opposite directions. It can be argued that this was fortuitous. Had it not been for a convergence of developments toward the end of 1983, Soviet-American relations might have entered a new phase before Gorbachev became General Secretary.

On the last day of August, Soviet air defense forces in the Far East shot down a Korean Air Lines passenger jet that had strayed into Soviet air space. It was one of those incidents, like the Soviet downing of the American U-2 spy plane in 1960, that periodically derail Soviet-American relations. Quiet diplomacy of the sort that Shultz was attempting was no longer the order of the day. Reagan had been scheduled for some time to address the United Nations General Assembly. He condemned what the Soviets had done in the harshest terms and denounced the U.S.S.R. as an international outlaw. In early September, Shultz met with the Gromyko in Madrid, again for a long-planned session, and was treated to a *tour de force* of aggressive unrepentance. Gromyko not only refused to acknowledge any Soviet wrongdoing in the affair, he tried to blame the United States for this latest crisis. He claimed, in effect, that the Korean jet was a kind of U-2 in civilian disguise, and that it deserved what it got.

Meanwhile, Andropov, who was officially said to be suffering from a "cold," was in fact dying. Over the years, when the first among equals in Moscow had been incapacitated, his colleagues not only functioned entirely by consensus, but the center of gravity within that consensus had shifted toward unyielding opposition to the United States. There seems to be a deeply ingrained fear that the enemies of the Soviet Union, principally the United States, will move to exploit any perceived weakness at a time of uncertainty or transition; therefore the collegium must not merely close ranks but demonstrate its toughness. This phenomenon was particularly evident in late 1983, in the absence of a vigorous, or even functional, leader. Having set a hard line in response to the Ronald Reagan of 1981–82, the Soviets were not going to moderate it for the George Shultz of 1983.

In addition, the United States and the Soviet Union were on a collision course over the deployment of American missiles due in Western Europe at the end of 1983. The Soviets had repeatedly threatened to walk out of the negotiations if the deployments began on schedule. The Soviets were clearly hoping that the West Europeans would be sufficiently unhappy at that prospect to put pressure on the United States at least to postpone deployment. By autumn it was clear that Moscow had badly miscalculated. The American missiles would be deployed on schedule. Having painted themselves into a corner, the Soviets had to sit there. So they did, for almost a year, all the while blaming the United States for the breakdown in relations.

On September 28, 1983, the Soviet media published one of the more extraordinary statements in the annals of superpower relations. It seemed to be nothing less than formal notice that the leadership of the Soviet Union was giving up on further attempts at constructive diplomatic engagement with the United States so long as the incumbent President was in office. Amidst invective about "the outrageous militarist psychosis" and the "imperial ambitions" of the United States, one sentence in particular stood out, attracting wide comment both by Western analysts and by Soviet commentators:

> If anyone had any illusions about a possible evolution for the better in the policy of the present American Administration, such illusions have been finally dispelled by the latest developments.

The key word in the sentence was "finally." It suggested that a final determination had been made and that the debate was over. While the statement was released in Andropov's name, its publication came amidst mounting speculation that the General Secretary was seriously, perhaps terminally, ill. Some sources in Moscow, believed to be associated with Andropov's alma mater, the KGB, put the story out that the "no-illusions" passage was actually self-critical: Andropov himself had been the only one still nurturing such illusions in the fall of 1983; the Korean airliner affair and the impending deployment of the American Euromissiles had caused the scales to fall even from his trusting eyes. For the KGB to be fostering such rumors while its old leader was still alive strongly suggested that he was so sick that he was unable to move against his enemies; it also suggested that the intramural maneuvering for the succession had begun.

Foreign Ministry officials, meanwhile, urged readers to pay close attention to the end of the statement, where Andropov was quoted as saying that despite all that had gone before, the U.S.S.R. would continue the search for peace:

> Mankind has not lost, nor can it lose, its reason. This is clearly manifested by the great scope of the anti-missile, anti-war movement which has developed on the European and other continents, a movement in which people of different social, political, and religious affiliations participate. All who raise today their voice against the senseless arms race and in defense of peace can be sure that the policy of the Soviet Union, and of other socialist countries, is directed at attaining precisely these aims. The U.S.S.R. wants

to live in peace with all countries, including the
United States. It does not nurture aggressive plans,
does not impose the arms race on anybody, does not
impose its social order on anyone. Our aspirations
and strivings are implemented in concrete proposals
directed at effecting a decisive turn for the better in
the world situation. The Soviet Union will continue
to do everything possible to uphold peace on earth.

It was, as Russians like to say, no accident that
Soviet diplomats in Western Europe particularly
urged officials of their host governments to pay special heed to this passage. The implication was that
even if the Kremlin had given up on doing business
with Washington, it was, if anything, all the more
eager to work with Bonn, Brussels, the Hague,
Rome, London and Paris. The statement reflected
what Andropov's healthier colleagues saw as a necessary part of their strategy: to find a way to use the
breakdown in their own relations with the United
States to stir up trouble between America and its
allies.

In the short term, that tactic failed. A few weeks
after the September 28 statement, when the first
American missiles arrived in Britain and West Germany, the Soviet negotiators pulled out of the talks in
Geneva. The walkout came no closer to splitting the
alliance than the threat of one had done during the
previous two years. If anything, the effect was doubly disadvantageous to the Soviets: the Reagan Administration, along with the conservative governments of Britain and West Germany, appeared the
victors in a battle of wills with the U.S.S.R. over
deployment; and the Soviets were made to seem the

childish spoilers, putting false pride ahead of the search for peace.

Like the September 28 philippic released in Andropov's name, the statement that the Soviets' chief negotiator in Geneva read as he walked out of the talks was the product of committee draftsmanship. Gorbachev was unquestionably part of the committee. He was thus very much associated with a Kremlin policy toward the United States that was a mirror image of what Washington had been trying to do to the Soviet Union in 1981: isolating it and blaming it for conduct unbecoming a superpower.

The most dramatic manifestation of the Soviets' pique was their boycott of the 1984 summer Olympics in Los Angeles, announced in early May. This was more than a gesture on their part. They were denying themselves a chance to instill pride at home and to demonstrate their superiority in an international arena in which their youth could compete with the West's. In 1980 the Carter Administration had boycotted the Moscow Olympics in protest over the invasion of Afghanistan. Still smarting from that reprisal in 1984, the Kremlin saw an opportunity for simple revenge. What it failed to see was an opportunity to contrast its own international good citizenship with the spoil-sport behavior of the Americans four years before. By leading a boycott, the Soviets paid a price not only in international prestige but also in resentment on the part of their fraternal neighbors, particularly the athletically prodigious East Germans, who had to stay home.

Meanwhile, Soviet spokesmen, in public and in private, were offering a bleak assessment of the chances for any kind of improvement in the Soviet-

American relationship. American analysts debated whether all of these outbursts of Soviet displeasure were "strategic" or "tactical." Was the Kremlin battening down for a long period of confrontation and tension with the United States, while maneuvering for political and propaganda advantages, particularly with Western Europe? Or was Moscow prepared to do business with the Reagan Administration if and when there was business to be done? And were Soviet proclamations of gloom and doom, such as Andropov's, nothing more than pressure tactics to get the United States to negotiate seriously all the sooner and on Soviet terms? Officials and supporters of the Reagan Administration tended toward the view that the Soviet snit was purely tactical; critics of the Administration policy tended to accept, and in some ways adopt, Soviet pessimism as their own.* In the near—and perhaps in the middle—term, events provided more evidence to support the former than the latter view.

The year 1984 did see some adjustments on both sides, but the effect was tentative and confusing. Not only were American presidential election-year politics weighing on American foreign policy, but the Soviet leadership was undergoing one succession even as it prepared for another.

---

*One pessimist was Professor Seweryn Bialer of Columbia University, who, on returning from a visit to Moscow at the beginning of 1984, wrote that the Politburo had "concluded that any attempt to improve relations would be futile" and that the Soviet leaders might be tempted into more dangerous gambles ("Kremlin, Insecure, Might Increase Risks," *The New York Times*, February 5, 1984).

American politics prompted a softer Administration line toward the Soviet Union. Reagan's pollsters told him that the only issue on which he was even slightly vulnerable to the Democrats was "peace," meaning the deterioration of Soviet-American relations and the stalemate in arms control. Reagan's advisers Stuart Spencer, James Baker and Michael Deaver, with the support of Mrs. Reagan, persuaded the President that he must blunt the Democrats' attempt to portray him as an intransigent anti-Soviet warrior. On January 16, 1984, Reagan delivered a relatively conciliatory speech, later published under the title "Realism, Strength and Dialogue." "Neither we nor the Soviet Union can wish away the differences between our two societies and our philosophies," he said:

> But we should always remember we do have common interests. . . . There is no rational alternative but to steer a course which I would call credible deterrence and peaceful competition.

The contrast with the rhetoric of three years before could hardly have been sharper. A few days later, on January 24, another pronouncement from Andropov cautiously and grudgingly echoed the Reagan call for a dialogue. That was to be virtually his last public pronouncement. On February 9, he died of acute kidney failure. His successor, Chernenko, was very much the lowest-common-denominator candidate and obviously a caretaker. His meager claim to office was based on long and faithful service as Brezhnev's right-hand man during the heyday of détente. That experience may have predisposed him to at least some improvement in Soviet-American relations. Later in the year, the political analysts of the Soviet Foreign Ministry, international-affairs institutes, and KGB apparently concluded that, their fervent hopes to the contrary notwithstanding, Reagan was certain to be re-elected. Therefore their government would be well advised to accept the inevitable and position itself to deal with the second Reagan term. In September, Gromyko visited Washington and met with the President. This gesture could be seen as the official abandonment of the Kremlin line laid down by the Andropov statement of September 1983. By calling at the White House, Gromyko was also widely interpreted to be casting the vote of Andropov's successors for Reagan—not, of course, out of preference, but out of their "scientific analysis of objective reality" (a phrase common in Soviet discourse, especially at that time).

However, concrete negotiation in 1984 was difficult, because of both Reagan's preoccupation with his campaign and Chernenko's lack of personal standing and power base (not to mention physical energy) to launch significant initiatives. His heart condition and emphysema soon proved almost as incapacitating as Andropov's kidney ailments. Reagan dealt with the political challenge facing him far more easily than Chernenko was able to cope with his medical problems. Less than two months after Reagan's inauguration at the beginning of 1985, Chernenko died and Gorbachev became General Secretary. His formal assumption of that post was not a surprise. He had long been regarded as the heir apparent and had been acting as regent for some months during Chernenko's final illness. Thus the beginning of Reagan's second term roughly coincided with Gorbachev's emergence as leader of the U.S.S.R.

Soviet-American relations had entered a new phase. Well before their historic first meeting in November 1985, a highly personalized rivalry between the two men emerged. Reagan and Gorbachev altered the tone of the relationship. They did so largely in response to each other. After four years of dealing, or not dealing, with a geriatric and largely unseen Kremlin leadership, Reagan now had to contend with an energetic, ambitious and much younger opposite number. It quickly became apparent that here was a Soviet leader who, even though he had been involved in the Kremlin's angry withdrawal in 1983–84, would not indulge in walkouts and boycotts now that he was fully in charge. It could be surmised that he had become leader of the Soviet Union partly because the other members of the Politburo wanted somebody who could be seen as a match for the American President, and who could stay in the ring with him.

The U.S. press and some of the President's advisers depicted the Reagan-Gorbachev meeting as a title match, the champ versus the challenger, the Old Man versus the Kid. The Soviets, too, played on a variation on this pugilistic theme. At conferences and in interviews, Soviet spokesmen enjoyed challenging their American interlocutors with rhetorical questions: Now which superpower was led by a septuagenarian? And which leadership could claim to be characterized by youth and vigor? But these same Soviets clearly had another hope: that Gorbachev's ascendance would permit a new degree of continuity and progress in state-to-state relations. This hope was shared by some in Washington. A number of White House and State Department officials noted that Reagan, too, preferred a "one-on-one" approach to statesmanship; he wanted a counterpart with whom he could "engage"; he wasn't just spoiling for a fight—he was eager to "do business with someone over there." And so he went to Geneva to see what he could do.

A NEW CIVILITY, BUT OLD GOALS

There was a dramatic change of style in the second Reagan term, and the President's participation in the Geneva summit meeting was the most emphatic example of that change. His rhetoric was cooler. His statements after his second inaugural echoed the "peace campaign" he had waged in 1984; they were a far cry from the comments had had made four years earlier, in his opening press conference as President, when he said that the Soviets "reserve unto themselves the right to commit any crime, to lie, to cheat to obtain [the goal of world Communism]." He avoided referring to the Soviet Union as an "evil empire," a phrase he had used in a speech on March 8, 1983, to the National Association of Evangelicals in Orlando, Florida. There were other examples of this new tone as well. In the same speech, Reagan had argued that the contest between the superpowers is "the struggle between right and wrong and good and evil," and emphatically *not* "a giant misunderstanding." Yet in a number of his statements during his second term, Reagan came very close to describing the conflict as, precisely, a misunderstanding, based on mutual suspicions that could, through summitry and negotiation, be largely dispelled.

He moved toward this position gradually. On March 11, 1985, the day that Gorbachev's selection was announced in Moscow, Reagan told a group of newsmen, "There's a great mutual suspicion between the two countries. I think ours is more justified than theirs." But as the summit grew closer, Reagan seemed more willing to give Gorbachev the benefit of the doubt. In an interview with the BBC on October 30, he said that the meeting would be a success "if we could eliminate some of the paranoia, if we could reduce the hostility, the suspicion that keeps our two countries. . .at odds with each other. . . .If we can reduce those suspicions between our two countries, the reduction of arms will easily follow because we will have reduced the feeling that we need them." A few days later, on November 12, he went even further with a group of foreign broadcasters. He said he was looking forward to meeting Gorbachev "one-on-one" in order to "eliminate the suspicion. . .that we mean him harm." Immediately after the summit, he went further still. "I think I'm a good judge of acting," said the President. "I don't think he was acting. He, I believe, is just as sincere as we are."

In fact, there was less significance in the change in rhetoric than met the ear. Reagan toned down the invective for a variety of reasons that had little to do with any change in his perceptions or convictions and a great deal to do with what the moment required and his sense of what would please his audience. Like most politicians, he had a tendency to tell people what they wanted to hear. When addressing fundamentalist Christians in Florida, he naturally spoke of the Manichean struggle between the forces of light and the forces of darkness. When appearing at a joint press conference with the Soviet leader in Geneva, after what had generally been regarded not merely as a successful meeting but as a personal triumph for Reagan himself, it was natural that he would dwell on the benefits of the meeting and the need for more.

When asked why he had dropped any reference to the evil empire, Reagan was disarmingly candid and unrepentant. On March 24, 1986, he told Barbara Walters of ABC News:

> I have tactfully tried to quiet down now because we are trying to talk and arrive at some agreements. I do not regret at all saying those things. . .I thought it was necessary to establish reality; to let them see that, no, we definitely saw what they were doing as evil. . .I wanted them to know that I saw them realistically.

The softening of Presidential rhetoric and the partial restoration of some aspects of détente were obviously a change from the initial Reagan policy toward the Soviet Union. But speeches, meetings with the Soviet leader, and arms-control negotiations were only part of Soviet-American relations. In other ways American policy was moving in quite a different direction, toward an intensification of the confrontation.

The procedures of détente had developed in recognition, as the Soviets saw it, of an underlying condition. That condition was the Soviet Union's attainment of the status of the international equal of the United States. That status, in turn, rested on a series of Soviet achievements over four decades. The first and probably the most important achievement, the one on which the Soviet position in the world depended most heavily, was strategic nuclear parity, which the weapons programs of the 1950s and 1960s had made possible.* The second was the Soviet empire in Central and Eastern Europe, acquired in World War II and maintained thereafter by a Soviet garrison and occasional interventions. The third and most recent achievement was the expansion of Soviet influence beyond Europe to the far corners of the Third World, where Moscow had, mainly in the 1970s, collected a series of allies, clients and dependents.

These three accomplishments were, in the Soviet view, international facts of life. Various diplomatic byproducts of détente served—again, from the Soviet perspective—as validations of those realities by the world community in general, and by the United States in particular. Moscow could claim that the division of Europe, and Soviet hegemony over its eastern half, had been ratified by the Final Act of the Conference on European Security and Cooperation, one of Brezhnev's pet projects, signed in Helsinki in 1975. Strategic nuclear parity was embodied in the ongoing arms-control negotiations and in the SALT agreements of 1972 and 1979. There was no comparable charter for the Soviet presence in the Third World, but the United States had, by and large, refrained from vigorously challenging these new footholds of Soviet power during the heyday of détente. Weariness from the long and unsuccessful war in In-

---

*The same period also saw huge increases in Soviet conventional forces in the Eurasian heartland and in the ability to project power overseas.

dochina had a great deal to do with American reticence in this regard. The Soviets were well aware of the "Vietnam syndrome." On the one occasion when the Executive Branch had tried to contest a Soviet gain in the Third World, by aiding the anti-Soviet faction in the Angolan civil war in 1974, Congress had intervened to tie the Administration's hands.

As Moscow saw it, all three of these achievements—strategic nuclear parity, the domination of Eastern Europe, and the establishment of client regimes in the Third World—were both legitimate and permanent. Reagan, however, held a different view; he considered these Soviet achievements neither legitimate nor permanent. His Administration embarked on policies that challenged each of them.

"ROLLBACK" IN EUROPE

Reagan made his challenge to the Soviet position in Europe most directly in a speech to the British Parliament on June 9, 1982. He urged the West to launch "a crusade for freedom." The effort would not, he strongly implied, be just a war of words, nor would it be simply a matter of harassing Soviet power around the fringes of its far-flung empire. "We must take actions to assist the campaign for democracy," he said. Reagan seemed to be suggesting a strike deep behind enemy lines—that the United States, in concert with its more strong-willed allies, should undermine Soviet power within the East Bloc and, if possible, within the U.S.S.R. itself.

In his speech to the British Parliament, Reagan repeatedly quoted its pre-eminent twentieth-century

son, Winston Churchill. He wanted above all to iden-
tify himself with the Churchill who had coined the
term "Iron Curtain," whose ringing phrases had ush-
ered in the Cold War, and who had warned the West
to oppose the Soviet takeover of Eastern Europe.
Reagan seemed to break with the orthodoxy of the
1960s and 1970s, which had accepted the Soviet Empire; he wanted more than containment, which conceded to the Soviets gains they had already made; he
favored something like "rollback," and, insofar as rollback ended at the borders of the U.S.S.R., he seemed
even to want something more ambitious than that.*

Reagan noted that totalitarian regimes had already
had more than three decades in which to establish

---

*The word "rollback" had been used by John Foster
Dulles, among others, to mean undermining and if possible
overthrowing Communist regimes in Asia and Eastern Europe. Significantly, Dulles championed it in the late 1940s,
especially after the Communist coup d'état in Czechoslovakia, and early 1950s during the Korean war—*before* he became Secretary of State.

Another telling incident occurred during Reagan's first
term when an official of the United States Information
Agency, Scott Thompson, gave a series of supposedly off-
the-record lectures, some of them to audiences of U.S. military officers, saying that the world had moved into the
"post-containment era," and it was time to "take the struggle directly to the enemy, on his own ground." When word
leaked that an Administration official was talking this
way—even though he was not at the highest level—Soviet
analysts of the American scene reacted with dismay. They
were similarly upset when, sometime later, a spate of artic-
les appeared that called into question whether the Yalta
Agreement of World War II did in fact constitute Western
acceptance of perpetual Soviet hegemony over Eastern Europe. See particularly Zbigniew Brzezinski, "The Future
of Yalta," *Foreign Affairs*, Winter 1984/85.

themselves "from Stettin on the Baltic to Varna on the Black Sea" (with this variation of the phrase Churchill had made famous in Fulton, Missouri, at the outbreak of the Cold War, Reagan excluded Yugoslavia from the ranks of captive nations); "but none—not one regime—has yet been able to risk free elections. Regimes planted by bayonets do not take root."

The idea of Communism's being rejected by its own subjects went back to Reagan's experience during his campaign for the presidency in 1976, when he had run against, and only narrowly lost to, his fellow Republican Gerald Ford. That sometimes bitter contest had featured a flap over the so-called Sonnenfeldt Doctrine. It played only a minor role in the politics of that year, but, according to some of Reagan's associates, it had an important and lasting impact on the future President.

In December 1975, Helmut Sonnenfeldt, an experienced Sovietologist in the inner circle of Henry Kissinger, addressed an off-the-record seminar of American diplomats in London. His thesis was that European stability was endangered by the chronic strains between the Soviet Union and the nations that it dominated in Eastern Europe: East-West relations were complicated by East-East relations. The failure of the Communist regimes to establish what he called an "organic" relationship between subjects and subjugators created an ever-present danger of conflict within the East bloc; that danger, in turn, carried with it the danger of a broader conflict involving the West. Sonnenfeldt's point anticipated Reagan's of six years later: "Regimes planted by bayonets do not take root." But that was not the interpretation his ruminations received when a classified State Department cable reporting on the London meeting was leaked to the syndicated columnists Rowland Evans and Robert Novak in March 1976. They wrongly accused Sonnenfeldt of saying that the West must tolerate and even foster Soviet domination of Eastern Europe on the grounds that "permanent 'organic' union between the Soviet Union and Eastern Europe is necessary to avoid World War Three."

This supposed "doctrine" was widely attacked by conservatives as a pernicious corollary of détente. A few days after the revelation of Sonnenfeldt's remarks, Reagan delivered a televised address saying that Sonnenfeldt and the Administration he worked for believed that "the captive nations should give up any claim of national sovereignty and simply become a part of the Soviet Union."*

In 1980 one of Reagan's own advisers remarked that Reagan was "itching for the chance to reverse, once and for all, the perfidious Sonnenfeldt Doctrine and to demonstrate that, as far as he was concerned, the ultimate fate of Eastern Europe has yet to be decided." Clearly, any doctrine that a Reagan Administration proclaimed would be a vigorous repudiation of what Sonnenfeldt was supposed to have said.

---

*Ford inadvertently confused the issue further during the general election campaign in the fall. In a debate with Jimmy Carter, Ford asserted, "There is no Soviet domination of Eastern Europe, and there never will be under a Ford Administration." He meant, of course, that he did not *accept* Soviet domination of the East bloc, but it sounded as though he did not acknowledge it as a reality. An incredulous journalist on the panel gave him a chance to clarify, but Ford bulled ahead: "Each of these countries is independent, autonomous."

By 1982, when he addressed the British Parliament, President Reagan's attraction to the idea of the eventual emancipation of Eastern Europe drew additional force from events then taking place in Poland. The independent trade-union movement had been outlawed and many of its leaders jailed. The nation was under martial law. While this state of affairs could hardly be seen as auspicious for Lech Wałęsa and Solidarity, it was also a tacit admission of the failure of the Soviet system and the Polish Communist Party. The armed forces had, at Moscow's behest, in effect carried out a coup d'état against the Party. To what extent the authorities could politically neutralize Solidarity remained to be seen. Reagan, like many others, may have hoped that the Soviet-ordered crackdown in Poland would prove to be the beginning of a new era of sustained and ultimately successful resistance to Soviet rule *within the Soviet camp.* He came very close to saying as much in his speech to Parliament, and there were intriguing if vague suggestions that the West could help foster that success:

> In the Communist world. . .man's instinctive desire for freedom and self-determination surfaces again and again. To be sure, there are grim reminders of how brutally the police state attempts to snuff out this quest for self-rule—1953 in East Germany, 1956 in Hungary, 1968 in Czechoslovakia, 1981 in Poland. But the struggle continues in Poland. *And we know that there are even those who strive and suffer for freedom within the confines of the Soviet Union itself. How we conduct ourselves here in the Western democracies will determine whether this trend continues.* No, democracy is not a fragile flower. Still it needs cultivating. If the rest of

this century is to witness the gradual growth of freedom and democratic ideals, we must take actions to assist the campaign for democracy. . .We cannot ignore the fact that even without our encouragement there has been and will continue to be repeated explosions against repression and dictatorships. *The Soviet Union itself is not immune to this reality. Any system is inherently unstable that has no peaceful means to legitimize its leaders. In such cases, the very repressiveness of the state ultimately drives people to resist it, if necessary, by force.* [Italics added.].

All previous postwar Presidents had considered the Soviet preserve in Central and Eastern Europe illegitimate. They could hardly have thought otherwise, since the peoples of that region made plain their feelings through periodic uprisings against Soviet-imposed rule. But Eisenhower had declined to assist the Hungarians in 1956, and Johnson kept the United States very much on the sidelines during the Prague Spring and the Soviet invasion of Czechoslovakia in 1968. While Reagan refused to intervene in Poland in 1981, his speech to Parliament was as close as any American President had come to endorsing what might be called total rollback, or counterrevolution at the source, at least since Woodrow Wilson sent American troops to Russia during the Civil War of 1918-20. Reagan was encouraged not only by events in Poland but by the views of some of his personal advisers, notably Richard Pipes, a Harvard professor of history and the principal Soviet-affairs authority on the staff of the National Security Council. Pipes believed that the Soviet system had failed to acquire legitimacy in the eyes of its own subjects; that it was, accordingly, vulnerable to eruptions of their discontent; and that the West would have opportunities in the years ahead to induce internal changes in the U.S.S.R.*

Reagan's theme in his address to Parliament broke with what had been the principal U.S. attitudes toward the Soviet Union since World War II, and especially in the previous decade. Some found the speech refreshing, others found it alarming, and almost everyone found it an interesting expression of Reagan's general view of the world; but very few in the West took it seriously *as a statement of policy*. It was heady stuff, generating a predictable mixture of applause, controversy and protest; but it did not have much impact on the foreign-policy community. There was little follow-up in the form of cables from the State Department, Pentagon or Central Intelligence Agency with instructions on how to implement the President's vision.

The speech was soon undercut by the course of events. The struggle between the Polish regime and Solidarity turned out to be a one-sided contest, and, for those watching in the West, a discouraging one. Nor was there any sign of the Polish phenomenon spreading to East Germany or to the Soviet Union itself, as some had expected and many had hoped.

Moreover, the Reagan Administration's efforts to take even modest measures to capitalize on Soviet troubles within the Eastern bloc had little success. Any attempt to change the status quo in Central and

*For a detailed analysis of the Soviet system and set of recommendations for a U.S. "policy designed to assist from the outside the forces that make for change internally," see Pipes, *Survival Is Not Enough* (New York: Simon and Schuster, 1984).

Eastern Europe required the active participation of the West Europeans, who showed no interest in any kind of anti-Soviet campaign. Their insistence that the American government negotiate with the Soviets on the issue of the Euromissiles that were scheduled to be deployed in 1983 was one illustration of this attitude. Another was their response to the suppression of Solidarity. Washington sought to enlist the West European leaders in a program of economic sanctions. They refused, putting the American government in an embarrassing bind. Doing nothing made the West look weak; but efforts at coordinated initiatives against the Soviet Union failed, and that failure threatened to undermine Western unity. Instead of highlighting and exploiting the limits of Moscow's control over its own bloc, the American undertaking inadvertently dramatized the limits of the United States' influence over its own allies.

The President sensed that he had gone too far, that he needed to tone down his rhetoric about the division of Europe and adopt more attainable objectives. He knew that there was a risk of raising expectations that he could not fulfill and of arousing anxieties that he could not allay.

By the time Reagan departed for his Geneva summit meeting with Gorbachev in late 1985, he had begun denying any desire to alter the Soviet system. "We don't like their system," he told the BBC in October 1985. "They don't like ours. But we're not out to change theirs." A few days later, he told a group of foreign broadcasters, "As I've said before, we're not trying to change their system internally." There were no more hints at a Western campaign to loosen the Soviet grip on its East European satellites.

Nonetheless, Reagan continued to favor stepping up the superpower rivalry. "There isn't any reason why we can't co-exist in the world," he said in his BBC interview before the Geneva summit, adding "Where there are legitimate areas of competition, [we should] compete." Similarly, in his interview with the foreign broadcasters, he had said, "What I think it's necessary to do is to let them know that the democratic world is not going to hold still for their expansionism into other parts of the world and to our own countries."

By then, he had found a way to redefine "legitimate areas of competition" in such a way as to make a geopolitical offensive against the Soviet Union more feasible. His rhetoric would be less provocative. He would no longer threaten to bring the walls of the Kremlin crashing down. But he was not about to accept everything that had been acceptable to Nixon, Ford and Carter. Perhaps the Soviets' gains of the 1940s were beyond the power of the United States to reverse, but their gains of the 1970s in Asia, Africa and Latin America were a different matter. These were fair game. These the President proposed to contest.

THE REAGAN DOCTRINE

The expansion of Soviet influence into the Third World during the 1970s took a new and, from the American standpoint, ominous form. It involved the imposition and maintenance of Soviet-style regimes in countries far from the U.S.S.R., and in some instances close to the United States. This Soviet policy amounted to the export not only of revolution but of replicas of the political, military and security apparatus of the Soviet Union itself.

Soviet interest in the world outside Europe had a checkered history. Stalin paid little attention to regions beyond the reach of his tanks; his principal concern was to establish a buffer zone around the Soviet Union. His successors looked further afield not because they were more ambitious but because there were greater opportunities in the 1950s. The decolonization of much of the Third World seemed to invite Communist revolution and Soviet penetration. Khrushchev foresaw extensive gains by the Soviet Union among the peoples newly freed from colonial rule or engaged in "wars of national liberation." During his rule, Moscow made political and economic investments and cultivated nationalist leaders in Indonesia, Egypt, Guinea, Ghana, the Congo and Algeria. The results, however, were disappointing to the Soviets. Some of the men on whose fidelity the Kremlin depended broke with Moscow; others were either forced from power or failed to advance Soviet goals. The Third World leader who proved the most stubbornly independent, and at great cost to the Soviet Union, was Mao Zedong.

The one successful Soviet venture outside Europe in the 1960s was Cuba, and the pattern there served as a model for the expansion of Soviet influence a decade later. Although they differed from one another, Moscow's connections with Vietnam, South Yemen, Syria, Libya, Ethiopia, Angola, Mozambique and Nicaragua have certain features in common with the Soviet-Cuban relationship. Like Cuba, these countries entered the Soviet orbit through the initiative of local factions which seized power and then turned to Moscow in their quest to consolidate power. The most important connection in all cases was military. The arms that the Soviets could offer counted for much more than any kind of ideological solidarity.

Fearful that their clients of the 1970s would go their own ways, as had the nationalist leaders of the 1950s and 1960s, Soviet officials encouraged the establishment in the newly acquired client countries of what might be called "Leninist franchises." They tried to foster the full panoply of Communist institutions: an all-powerful Communist Party (whether by that or some other name) with a small ruling group at the top; the suppression of all other independent centers of authority (opposition political parties, religious groups, and labor unions); strict censorship; a large, powerful internal security service; and a central planning and management apparatus to oversee the entire national economy, including agriculture.

Cuba began to equip itself with a full-scale Leninist political structure in the mid-1960s. The Soviets' dependents of the 1970s and 1980s have followed this model to varying degrees. Ethiopia has established a Communist Party, imported a full complement of East German security advisers, and moved to organize agriculture in collective fashion. (This last measure has exacerbated a devastating famine, much as Stalin's collectivization of agriculture did in Russia in the 1930s.)

From the point of view of the Soviet leadership, the results of the experience of the 1970s have been mixed. By planting their flag on every continent, the Soviets can claim to be a global power. But the process of collecting this particular group of clients has strained relations with the United States. Once again, Cuba established an important precedent in this regard. The embattled island was the site, in 1962, of the single most dangerous confrontation between the superpowers. While nothing like the Cuban missile crisis has occurred since then, Soviet successes in Africa and Asia have helped to derail the relationship with the Americans that Brezhnev thought he had established in the early 1970s. After Soviet and Cuban military assistance helped Ethiopia drive Somalian forces from the Ogaden Desert that forms the contested border between Ethiopia and Somalia, Zbigniew Brzezinski, Carter's national security adviser remarked, "Détente perished in the sands of the Ogaden."

The associates and dependents that the Kremlin assembled, moreover, were frequently troublesome and embarrassing and, on occasion, downright dangerous for Moscow. Communist Afghanistan was in effect the city-state of Kabul under siege from the surrounding countryside. The Soviet defense of the Afghan puppet regime diverted more than 100,000 Soviet troops and cost 20–25,000 Soviet casualties since the initial Soviet intervention in December 1979. South Yemen erupted in a tribal civil war in early 1986. Syria (whose leaders' ties to Moscow did not stop them from harassing and executing local Communists) was prone to military engagements with its neighbor, Israel. That conflict risked dragging the Soviet Union into direct confrontation with the United States.

The members of the Soviet Union's outer empire were almost all poor; the more Leninist they became the more economically deprived they tended to be.

This pattern was not unknown within the Eastern bloc itself. Because these countries were poor, they wanted economic assistance from Moscow. Cuba had received a regular subvention since the 1960s, but there were signs that the Kremlin was balking at offering similar benefits to its new clients, regardless of how orthodox or destitute they were. Even before Gorbachev became General Secretary, official journals had published pieces expressing skepticism about the value of the new client states. In his speech to the Twenty-seventh Party Congress in 1986, Gorbachev barely mentioned the farthest outposts of Soviet influence and conspicuously avoided promising to assist them on a large scale.

However, while the Kremlin may have been rethinking the wisdom of acquiring new dependents, Gorbachev and his colleagues seemed determined not to retreat from those to whom they were already committed, particularly those under threat from the United States or its allies. When Israel humiliated Syria in the 1982 war in Lebanon, the Soviets quickly replenished Syrian military stockpiles and even improved the quality of the weapons they supplied. They stepped up their assistance to Cuba in the 1980s. In 1984 they increased their support for the Luanda regime in Angola, which was opposed by guerrillas who received encouragement and some material assistance from the United States.

Expensive and obscure though these clients undoubtedly were, they still had a certain value to the rulers of the Soviet Union. They showed that Marxism-Leninism was not simply a parochial Russian creation, that it could spread and, because it did spread, that the tides of history were favorable to the Communist cause. This idea helped to fortify the legitimacy of the Soviet regime at home.

Expansion beyond Europe also held the same attraction for the Soviet political class as had détente. It was a symbol of the Soviet Union's standing as the international equal of the United States, a badge of its status as the other superpower. The Americans had a network of friends, dependents and military bases all over the world; therefore the Soviet Union ought to have such a network as well. A comparison is sometimes drawn between the Soviet-American competition and the rivalry between Great Britain and Germany at the end of the nineteenth century. Britain, like the United States, was the leading power in the world, with a far-flung network of overseas possessions. Germany, like the Soviet Union, was the challenger, resentful of its rival's eminence and its extensive empire. Germany began to acquire colonies in part because Britain already had them; they were the mark of a great power. So it was with the Soviet Union a hundred years later. The outer empire was of no economic and only limited strategic value, but it was a form of conspicuous consumption, a geopolitical status symbol, a way of keeping up with the Joneses—or, in this case, with the Yankees.

It was this outer fringe of the Soviet empire that Reagan set out to challenge. His challenge was more than rhetorical, and it had more staying power than his abortive challenge to the Soviet position in Europe. By the time Mikhail Gorbachev came to power, it involved both weapons and men prepared to use them against armies and governments aligned with Moscow outside Europe. The series of initiatives that the Administration launched, and the guiding rationale for them, came to be known as the Reagan Doctrine.

The catch phrase "Reagan Doctrine" had been bandied about since before the beginning of the Reagan Administration. In the form that it ultimately took—active opposition to beleaguered Soviet client regimes outside Moscow's traditional orbit—the Reagan Doctrine was born on the beaches of Grenada in October 1983. American military forces, along with units from six Caribbean states, invaded Grenada ostensibly to rescue American medical students there and to end what the U.S. government called the "atmosphere of violent uncertainty" that had prevailed since a leftist regime had been replaced by an even more leftist one twelve days earlier. The episode was satisfying for the Reagan Administration for a number of reasons. The objective was clear and immediately attainable: to overthrow, with overwhelming force, the unpopular government of a tiny island in the Caribbean and to evict Moscow's minions. American television viewers were treated to the spectacle of Cuban advisers being marched off into captivity by GIs, and North Koreans being sent packing at the airport, some in tears of humiliation. Also, there was virtually no risk of touching off a broader war or of slipping into a direct confrontation with the Soviet Union.

By 1985, when Gorbachev emerged as the Soviet leader, Reagan had made it a cornerstone of his foreign policy that the United States would actively, and if necessary unilaterally, sponsor insurgencies seeking the overthrow of pro-Moscow leftist regimes in the Third World such as that in Grenada. The policy came into its own in his second term through the festering civil war in Nicaragua and the Administration's attempt to secure congressional support for the *contras*. This term was Spanish slang for "counterrevolutionaries," and counterrevolution in the Soviet camp was exactly what Reagan wanted to foster. That had been the essence of Reagan's opposition to Kissinger's policy of détente and its supposed corollary, the Sonnenfeldt Doctrine; it had been at the heart of his declaration of a rollback crusade; and it was central to the refined version of rollback that was to loom large in his second term. In addition to Nicaragua, Reagan targeted the Soviet client-governments of Ethiopia, Angola, Afghanistan and Cambodia.

In a series of speeches in the spring of 1985 he elaborated on a theme he had sounded in his State of the Union address in February:

> We must not break faith with those who are risking their lives on every continent from Afghanistan to Nicaragua to defy Soviet-supported aggression and secure rights which have been ours from birth. . . .Support for freedom fighters is self-defense.

The label "Reagan Doctrine" was given to this theme most firmly by the journalist and commentator Charles Krauthammer as the headline of an essay in *Time* Magazine.* Reagan's was not the first Administration to use the backing of anti-Soviet guerrillas as an instrument of American policy. In the Ford Administration, Kissinger had tried and failed to secure

Time, April 1, 1985. While Reagan did not refer to his policy as a doctrine bearing his own name, he and others in the Administration were delighted by the Krauthammer essay. For more than a year afterward, they frequently referred to it as the best explanation of what the Administration was trying to do and why.

congressional backing for covert American aid to a faction in the Angolan civil war that was fighting against the pro-Soviet Popular Movement for the Liberation of Angola. American assistance to the Islamic fundamentalists and nationalists who were resisting the Soviets in Afghanistan began under Jimmy Carter. But it was under Reagan that the policy of supporting such groups assumed unprecedented operational—and doctrinal—standing.

Reagan and his key advisers had long believed that one of the fatal flaws of détente was the notion that as a fellow superpower, the Soviet Union was entitled to have its client regimes around the world just as the United States did. Whatever euphemisms he might have adopted in the way he addressed the problem, he nonetheless believed that the Soviet Union was indeed both evil and an empire, that it did not deserve rights and privileges equal to those accorded the United States, and that to concede such rights and privileges would be both foolish and dangerous. Reagan believed, and his first-term ambassador to the United Nations, Jeane Kirkpatrick, helped him explain, that one of the principal differences between leftist totalitarian regimes and rightist authoritarian ones was that the first were more brutal and more firmly entrenched than the second; Moscow's dependents in the Third World were much less likely to be overthrown by internal opposition than regimes that the U.S. supported.*

*Reagan read Kirkpatrick's article "Dictatorships and Double Standards" in *Commentary*, November 1979, was impressed by her thesis, and chose her as his ambassador to the United Nations.

The twilight of the Carter Administration had provided vivid examples of both parts of the proposition: in Nicaragua, Anastasio Somoza, the son and heir of the tyrant whom Franklin Roosevelt had once described as "a son of a bitch, but *our* son of a bitch," was swept aside by the Sandinista revolution, while in Afghanistan, Angola, Cambodia, and Ethiopia, Soviet-backed regimes seemed capable of riding out both popular opposition and armed insurgency.

The Declaration of Principles that Nixon and Brezhnev signed at their summit meeting in Moscow in May 1972 contained a pledge that neither side would "seek unilateral advantage" against the other. One of the criticisms of détente was that the Soviet Union had made a mockery of that pledge by moving its advisers and its Cuban surrogates into Ethiopia and Angola, by supporting the Vietnamese invasion and occupation of Cambodia, and, most provocatively, by invading Afghanistan. Now the Reagan Administration proposed to turn the tables on the Soviet Union. From Khrushchev's time through Brezhnev's, Moscow had tried to convince Washington to accept the idea that there could, and should, be accommodation on such issues as arms control and trade even as the ideological struggle continued. Khrushchev tried to persuade Eisenhower that Soviet support for "national liberation movements" in no way contradicted his preferred policy of peaceful coexistence between the superpowers.

Now, under the Reagan Doctrine, the message of the American government was that it had both the right and the intention to seek unilateral advantages of its own, or at least to roll back the advantages the Soviets had seized in the 1970s. The United States would seek to alter the status quo in its own favor. In Rudyard Kipling's novel *Kim*, the rivalry between Britain and Russia in southwest Asia is called the Great Game. The Reagan Doctrine was an announcement that henceforth the United States would play the modern version of the game in spirited fashion, not to a draw but, in Lenin's famous term, as a matter of who would prevail over whom.

If Reagan's words in his second term had become softer, his policies, especially in the Third World, had become tougher. A pattern disturbing to the Soviet Union had emerged: the relative, tentative success of U.S. policy in El Salvador, followed by the military quick fix in Grenada; the more or less open campaign to oust the Sandinistas in Nicaragua; the doubling of aid to the Afghan rebels; a new front in Cambodia, modest enough in itself but conceivably the first step of an American return to Southeast Asia; and finally the reversal of American policy toward Angola, with stepped-up arms shipments and an all but public presidential embrace of the insurgent leader Jonas Savimbi. Taken together, these initiatives seemed to break the American losing streak that had begun with Vietnam, an outcome that was precisely what Reagan intended.

While the Administration's Nicaraguan policy remained highly controversial in the United States, the supposedly covert support for the Afghan and Cambodian insurgents received bipartisan support. This demonstrated that what *Pravda* and *Izvestia* called "sober forces" within the United States, which the Soviets had long seen as inhibiting American military action, were not as powerful as Moscow had hoped and believed.

Reagan's policies would have been unwelcome to the Kremlin at any time. But the 1980s were a particularly bad moment for him to have come along. The fortunes of the Soviet Union had fallen. Troubles at home preoccupied the new leader, but they were all the more pressing because of the challenge from abroad. Reagan's postwar predecessors had all been committed to trying to tame the Russian bear; he was prepared to kick it. This was bad enough for the Soviet leadership. What made matters worse from the Soviets' perspective was that Reagan was trying to kick them while they were down.

3

THE GORBACHEV AGENDA

When Leonid Brezhnev met Richard Nixon for the first time in Moscow in 1972, the Soviet Union was in the midst of the brightest period in its history. The leadership was unified. The economy was growing. The standard of living was rising: Soviet citizens were tolerably fed, and most were adequately housed. They wore better made clothing than in the past, and consumer goods, long a hallmark of the Western style of life, were beginning to be available. The country's borders were quiet. The Chinese were content to engage in verbal attacks rather than military skirmishes of the sort that had flared briefly in 1969. Czechoslovakia had been pacified. The Polish crisis, while simmering, had not yet reached a boil. There were problems, to be sure. The harvest, for example, was a particularly bad one. Still, the year 1972 was the midpoint of what can now be seen, in retrospect, as the golden decade of Soviet Communist rule. By the time that Mikhail Gorbachev met with Ronald Reagan in Geneva in 1985, all that had changed.

THE SOVIET CRISIS

Besides the difficulties for the Kremlin that the U.S. President was creating abroad under the banner of the Reagan Doctrine, the Soviet leadership faced mounting challenges at home. In the hierarchical Soviet system, when the man at the top cannot function, the gargantuan bureaucratic machine sputters. Direction, initiative and energy flow from the top down. The country had experienced at least half a decade of almost continual paralysis. In his last years Brezhnev had become "a semi-invalid who had difficulty remembering, hearing, and speaking clearly and who, some of the Soviet foreign policy establishment claim, was given to emotional breakdowns, with outbursts of weeping, in the course of ordinary Politburo sessions."* Yuri Andropov enjoyed a few months of health in power, but he was tethered to a kidney dialysis machine for the last part of his rule. Konstantin Chernenko was never vigorous, politically or physically, during his year as General Secretary.

The Soviet crisis was spiritual as well as political. Faith in the official ideology had long since evaporated. Nothing had arisen—nothing was permitted to arise—to take its place. Soviet society suffered from an almost total lack of optimism and civic enthusiasm. Partly for that reason the country was riddled with corruption. The illicit privileges that Brezhnev's family and cronies enjoyed toward the end of his life became an open secret in Moscow. Nor was it only the elite that flaunted the laws and rules of propriety.

*Timothy J. Colton, *The Dilemma of Reform in the Soviet Union*, 2d ed., (New York: Council on Foreign Relations, 1986), p. 26.

The underground economy was so far-reaching that the authorities could not have shut it down even if they had been so inclined. In fact they tolerated it not only because it was so deeply rooted in Soviet life but also because it helped to compensate for the chronic shortages of the official economy. Everyday corruption, however, went beyond such practices as exchanging a good cut of meat for a theater ticket, neither of which would be easily available otherwise. The theft of state property, such as construction materials, was rampant. It was widely considered acceptable, even normal. While paying lip service to state nostrums, managers were juggling the accounts of enterprises to meet state-ordered production quotas, and students, workers and neighbors were informing on each other. These practices were all part of the fabric of everyday life in the Soviet Union, the things Soviet citizens had to do simply to get along. The indicators of social well-being displayed disturbing trends in the 1980s. The rates of abortion, divorce, illegitimacy and alcoholism all climbed. Life expectancy, especially among Russian males, declined, a development without precedent in modern history for an industrial country not at war.

At the heart of the pervasive crisis that Gorbachev inherited were the difficulties of the Soviet economy. By the time he assumed power, the rate of economic growth had been in decline for two decades. It was an impressive 5.3 percent in the second half of the 1960s. It fell to 3.7 percent in the first half of the 1970s, 2.7 percent in the second half of that decade, and reached the 2 percent level in the early 1980s. A growth rate of 2 percent was not bad by the world's standards. But it was not only well below the level that the Soviet economy had achieved in the past, it was also considerably less than what the Soviet leaders believed they needed in the future. Just as discouraging from the Soviet point of view as the gross statistics was the state of high technology. The Soviet Union lagged far behind the West. The gap between it and the capitalist countries in microelectronics and computers, the key sectors for economic progress in the last years of the twentieth century, was wide and growing wider.

The Soviet economic difficulties affected other parts of Soviet society. They made the classic choice between guns and butter particularly acute. The leadership was committed to keeping up with the United States in the military field. The Soviet Union was believed by most Western observers to spend at least twice as large a percentage of its gross national product on defense as the United States. But if this meant sacrificing investment in social welfare and personal consumption, the leadership would pay a political price at home sooner or later.

Such legitimacy and popular support as the rulers enjoyed rested in large part on an unwritten social contract with the populace. The terms did not include political rights; on the contrary, the regime promised public order without dissent. But it did provide social benefits—health care, housing, old-age pensions, guaranteed jobs, and basic commodities at low prices if not high quality or in plentiful supply. These were meager and inadequate by Western standards, but they surpassed anything ever available in the U.S.S.R. before. In the 1960s and 1970s more and more Soviet citizens owned refrigerators, television sets, and even automobiles.

The declining rate of economic growth jeopardized that rising standard of living. It portended more shortages of everything, and shortages were bound to stimulate corruption and cynicism. With slow economic growth, the diet and therefore the health of the Soviet population would suffer. There was even the possibility that economic deterioration would lead to social disorder. In 1981 Konstantin Chernenko, then Brezhnev's closest colleague in the leadership, warned in language unusually strong for official commentary on such a subject that improper policies raised "the danger of social tension, of political and socioeconomic crisis."

Gorbachev could not evade the problem of economic stagnation. In the Soviet system the economy is entirely the responsibility of the political authorities. Brezhnev might blame the weather, Andropov the West, Gorbachev lazy workers and corrupt managers for the country's poor performance. Ultimately, however, the blame lay with the Party, and, specifically, with the Party leadership.

The principal cause of economic stagnation was clear to Western observers and apparently to many Soviet economists as well. The Soviet Union had relied since the 1930s on what economists call "extensive" growth, the increase of output by adding new factors of production—land, capital, labor and raw materials. Stalinist economic procedures lent themselves to the extensive method of economic growth. The command system could mobilize resources, especially human resources, on a large scale for a few major tasks such as building railroads, steel plants, and intercontinental ballistic missiles.

By the 1980s the pool of unused resources was depleted. Fewer workers could be drawn from the countryside to the cities to work in factories. No new sources of cheap energy were at hand. Economic progress would now have to come from the very different methods of "intensive" growth. Since Soviet planners could not easily increase their inputs, they had to find ways to use the inputs they had more efficiently. Their task, in the vocabulary of Western economics, was to increase productivity. There was also a pressing need for goods of higher quality.

These, however, were tasks to which the economic system Stalin had created and Gorbachev inherited was particularly ill-suited. Soviet economic mechanisms were neither flexible nor adaptable. They were not capable of the fine calculations and subtle adjustments on which increases in productivity and improvements in quality depend. The Soviet economy was a creature with strong thumbs but weak fingers. Such a system was poorly designed to make use of the new and increasingly indispensable technology of information-processing. The Soviet economy also lacked the single most important instrument of efficiency in capitalist countries, a realistic system of prices.

His country's economic difficulties posed a dilemma for Gorbachev. There was a way to improve the performance of the economy that was widely acknowledged if not publicly discussed even within the Soviet Union. Output could be increased by decentralizing authority. By giving individual workers, farmers, foremen, and managers more power over their own enterprises, Soviet authorities could get them to make more and better products. Reforms that permitted local decisions on what and how much to produce instead of having Moscow impose targets and quotas would, it was generally agreed, serve as a tonic for the Soviet economy.

But such reforms were bound to appear politically dangerous to the Soviet leadership. They would weaken the Party's grip on the country. They would dilute and perhaps even ultimately threaten Communist control in Russia and the other parts of the Soviet Union. They would subvert the first principle of Communist rule: All power to the Party. One of the great attractions of the Stalinist economic system to the Soviet authorities was that it was compatible with the Leninist style of politics. By the 1980s the Stalinist methods of managing the economy had outlived their usefulness. Yet Gorbachev and his colleagues did not regard the political system that had brought them to power as obsolete. Thus the traditional imperative of Soviet politics—Party power—was in conflict with the pressing requirements of the contemporary Soviet economy. It had remained a cardinal Communist rule since before 1917 that politics took priority over economics. Although he proposed modest experiments in decentralization, Gorbachev gave no hint that he would break that rule.

The difficulties were not, to be sure, as severe as those that the Bolsheviks faced in the Civil War following their seizure of power in 1917. Nor were the circumstances nearly as dire as they had been in 1942, when German armies occupied half of Russia. Gorbachev and his colleagues did not confront a crisis of survival. Communist control of Russia, the Ukraine, the Caucuses, Central Asia, and the Baltic republics was not in jeopardy. There was no prospect of disaffected workers and mutinous soldiers seizing the Kremlin in Moscow as a group of revolutionaries had stormed the Winter Palace in St. Petersburg almost seventy years before. The Soviet system retained vast reserves of stability, not the least of them the large and powerful internal security apparatus that stood ready to do the leaders' bidding.

The crisis, in the view of Seweryn Bialer, was one of effectiveness.* At stake was the capacity of the Soviet system to fulfill the promises that the leaders had made to the people and to achieve the goals that they had set for themselves. One of those goals was maintaining the international position that the Brezhnev generation had won. To hold it they needed, at the very least, an economy capable of producing the military hardware to keep up with the United States and the West.

Ronald Reagan's challenge to that position, coming in conjunction with the Soviet domestic economic troubles, made the task that Gorbachev confronted particularly urgent. He had to be concerned about the rising cost of supporting Soviet clients in Africa and Asia and the huge armies in Europe and on the border with China, as well as the price of the new round of competition in nuclear arms that the American President seemed to be threatening.

Gorbachev was well aware of the connection between foreign and domestic policy, and he made it one of the central themes of his public pronouncements. He exhorted his countrymen to do what was necessary for economic revival, not for their own benefit but for the sake of the Soviet Union's power and

*See his book *The Soviet Paradox: External Expansion, Internal Decline* (New York: Alfred A. Knopf, 1986), Part I.

prestige in the world. "The need to accelerate our socioeconomic development," he said soon after taking office, "is dictated by external circumstances. We are forced to put the necessary resources into the country's defense."

"There is a competition between two social systems, the socialist and the capitalist," he said on another occasion, which "obliges us to concern ourselves with accelerating our socioeconomic development." He found different ways to make the same point: "The main front in the struggle for peace lies in the resolution of the problems of improving socialist society. The definitive things are the condition of our economy, the development of science and technology, the qualitative restructuring of economic management, the building up of the spiritual, intellectual, and moral potential of the Soviet state." In a speech to selected Party leaders in December 1984, three months before he became General Secretary, Gorbachev expressed himself bluntly: What was at stake in the "titanic task" of energizing the Soviet economy and Soviet society, he told his listeners, was nothing less than the "ability of the Soviet Union to enter the new millennium in a manner worthy of a great and prosperous power." To remain a great power at the very least required sustaining military parity with the United States. Gorbachev's message to his countrymen was that parity begins at home.

In addition to putting a strain on the overall foreign policy of the Soviet Union, its domestic economic difficulties threatened serious international disadvantages. Backwardness in high technology had alarming implications for the non-nuclear military balance with the West. Future weapons were likely to rely increasingly on microelectronics, which would give them unprecedented accuracy. The Western armies in Europe were already beginning to incorporate these "emerging technologies."* The Warsaw Pact forces lagged well behind. Marshal Nikolai Ogarkov's forcefully stated dismay at Soviet shortcomings in this area were rumored to have caused his abrupt demotion from the post of Chief of the Soviet General Staff in 1984. Ogarkov was reported to have told the political authorities that they had to invest more in non-nuclear weaponry lest their European armies become dangerously vulnerable to the new Western armaments. Not liking what he had to say, or perhaps the way that he said it, the Kremlin oligarchs removed him.

The economic problems that Gorbachev inherited had another unhappy consequence. They made the Soviet system seem even less attractive and worthy of imitation to others, especially in the Third World where its offspring were already under fire from the Reagan Doctrine. This dimension of the problem, too, Gorbachev emphasized. The motherland of socialism, he said, "should also be a model of the highest organization and efficiency."

The Soviet leaders enjoyed a certain amount of international admiration by virtue of their status as the masters of the world's second-largest economy. In sheer size, however, if the trends of the early 1980s continued, the Soviet Union would soon be overtaken by Japan. The Soviet growth rate had also once been a source of respect; but in the 1970s the "Confu-

*On this subject see Andrew J. Pierre et al., *The Conventional Defense of Europe: New Technologies and New Strategies* (New York: Council on Foreign Relations, 1986).

cian" states of East Asia—Korea, Taiwan, and Singapore—had grown much more rapidly. There was also the troubling prospect of a resurgent China, its economy unleashed by the market reforms that Deng Xiaoping had introduced and growing at 5–7 percent per year in the 1980s. The Soviet leaders dared not try similar reforms for fear of losing their grip on the country. Soaring Chinese economic growth might ultimately pose a military threat to the Soviet Union if political relations between the two powers remained fractious. Successful Chinese reforms would have unwelcome political implications as well. They would discredit the Stalinist economic system by achieving success through deliberately discarding it and repudiating the country where that system had been born.

As the Soviet economy faltered, the Communist claim to the future rang increasingly hollow. In truth, however, it had sounded hollow for some time. The Soviet economic model had lost most of its appeal before Gorbachev became General Secretary. The crisis of the 1980s threw into sharp relief failings of the system that had long been apparent, even during the high point of the Brezhnev generation's confidence and success, in the midst of the Soviet golden decade.

Détente had, in the eyes of the Soviet leaders, meant international recognition of their country as the "other" superpower. But the country that they governed was a curious superpower indeed. In military might it was the equal of the United States, which set the standard for superpower status. In economic terms, however, the Soviet Union was not equal at all. Its gross national product was large, but the statistics describing its size hid as much as they revealed. Per capita gross national product was low. The quality of Soviet products was poor. A much larger proportion of the Soviet population was engaged in agriculture than in the West, yet the country still could not sustain the dietary levels to which the leadership was committed. The most technically sophisticated products remained beyond the capacity of Soviet scientists and engineers in the civilian sector to fashion, let alone of Soviet industry to manufacture on any appreciable scale. Although its military products were impressive, in other areas the Soviet economy had as much in common with the developing countries of the Third World as with the advanced capitalist states of North America, Western Europe and Japan.

In this respect the comparison between the Soviet-American rivalry and the competition between Britain and Germany at the turn of the century is illuminating for its contrasts rather than for its similarities. The Germans wanted what the British had—a large empire—just as the Soviet Union sought the same kind of global presence that the United States acquired after 1945. The Germans believed that they deserved what the British had. One reason for their sense of entitlement was that they had surpassed the British economically. With the most powerful, productive economy in Europe, the Germans wanted a political status commensurate with their economic achievements. The Soviet Union, by contrast, sought a political status far *exceeding* its economic achievements–indeed, despite its relative backwardness. The Brezhnev generation built a military colossus that bestrode half of Europe, but its foundations were weak.

It was not anchored solidly in either a thriving economy or a buoyant society.

Soviet economic weakness made a mockery of Andrei Gromyko's boast that "no question of any importance" could be decided "without the Soviet Union or in opposition to it." One of the most important international questions of the first half of the 1980s was the Third World debt crisis. A handful of large countries owed billions of dollars in loans to Western banks and, suffering from the effects of the recession of 1981–82, were unable to repay them on time. The problem fit easily into the Leninist analytic framework: The Western countries had exported their capital in search of high returns and were proposing to impoverish the workers and peasants of the Third World to assure their profits.

The Third World debtor nations demanded that the terms of their loans be softened. Extensive negotiations took place, complete with last-minute pledges of capital to avoid default. The International Monetary Fund, to which the Soviet Union did not belong, began to participate in what had begun as private transactions. Although they did receive concessions, the debtor countries were also forced to adopt measures that lowered the standard of living of their own people to keep up their payments.

In all of this the other superpower played virtually no role. The Soviet Union was not part of the prevailing economic system. It was the hub of a separate, but hardly flourishing, economic order. Even in this respect it was a negligible presence in the politics of international debt. Some of the Third World countries threatened not to pay. There was talk of a debtors' cartel. Yet none of these countries seriously considered repudiating its debts, leaving the capitalist system, and integrating its economy into the Soviet-centered Communist order. This was true even of Cuba, which was already part of the Communist economic framework but had nonetheless borrowed from Western banks. The Cubans urged others to repudiate their obligations; they themselves, however, kept up their payments. In theory the Soviet economic sphere stood as the logical alternative to the Western system, a refuge from that system's capitalists, banks, and international organizations that were applying pressure on debtor nations to endure hardships and make sacrifices. But for even the most desperate Third World government, the Communist bloc was so backward and stagnant that the prospect of forsaking the West to join it never even arose.

Marx had foreseen and Lenin had launched an economic competition between capitalism and socialism. By the time Lenin's political descendant Mikhail Gorbachev came to power, this competition had been decided in favor of the West. The chief aim of the socialist project, as its founders had understood it—the demonstrated superiority over capitalism of the socialist system in providing for the needs of its citizens—had failed.

Its failure was both a great advantage and a source of unending difficulty for the United States. It meant that in the global rivalry between them the Soviet Union was severely and perhaps permanently handicapped. There was simply no prospect that the Eastern bloc would ever be the equal of the international economic order that the United States led. But it also meant, for just that reason, that the Soviets, given their obsession with equality, would be perpetually dissatisfied with their international position. They would forever be seeking ways to compensate for their weaknesses at the expense of the West, inevitably through political subversion, military pressure or direct assault, which were their principal foreign-policy tactics.

Whatever Gorbachev's private views of Marx's doctrines and Lenin's aspirations, he did seem to recognize that Soviet economic failures jeopardized the geopolitical gains of his immediate predecessors. The close connection between vitality at home and success abroad was clear not just to him but to his colleagues as well. It was part of their basic outlook; indeed, it was central to their political vocabulary. The term "correlation of forces" has a prominent place in Soviet political discourse. It is a way of evaluating the strength of the competing powers in the international arena. The Soviets' preoccupation with the correlation of forces reflects their image of the world as a relentlessly competitive place; they are constantly measuring themselves against the West.

The Soviets define the correlation of forces broadly, more broadly than the comparison of arsenals that Western experts sometimes make when they try to assess the East-West balance. The correlation includes military power, of course, but also economic health, social cohesion, national unity and the strength of alliances. This more general concept of international strength than is common in the West is sometimes imputed to Lenin. It is certainly a properly Marxist idea, emphasizing as it does the social and economic basis of political power. But it is also a matter of experience and common sense. The conditions that comprise the correlation of forces are those that determine the outcome of major wars.

The correlation of forces as the Soviets define it includes, as comparable Western concepts often do not, the areas in which the Soviet Union trails the West. The Soviet leaders are aware of their weaknesses. The Brezhnev generation could take satisfaction in the conviction that where they lagged behind the West the gap was narrowing. The trends favored them. The official Soviet explanation for détente was that the United States had soberly recognized a new correlation of forces. What had changed most dramatically, of course, was the military component. But the Soviet Union was moving in the right direction in the other categories of national strength as well. Its economy was growing and its influence expanding, while the United States was in retreat from Asia, divided at home, and plagued by sharp rises in the price of oil. As the world's largest producer of petroleum, the U.S.S.R. had drawn considerable benefit from the leap in oil prices. But when Gorbachev assumed power, this was no longer the case. The trends in the correlation of forces were then running against the Eastern bloc.

In the days of sharpest tension between Moscow and Washington during the first Reagan term, Soviet spokesmen occasionally tried to blame their economic troubles on the West. They accused the Administration of setting out to cripple the Soviet economy by drawing the Soviet Union into a new and expensive round of the arms race. In fact, the basic cause of the country's economic woes lay closer to home. A joke circulating in Moscow made the point. Leonid Brezhnev, the story goes, is standing on Lenin's tomb during the May Day parade with a prominent foreign Communist at his side. The soldiers, tanks, airplanes and rockets pass in review. At the end of the procession comes a group of middle-aged men carrying briefcases. "Comrade Brezhnev," the foreign visitor asks, "who are those men?" "Those are our economists," his host replies. "But Comrade Brezhnev," the guest responds, "why, in a parade devoted to the military might of the Soviet Union, is a group of economists included?" "Ah," Brezhnev says, "You'd be surprised at how much damage they can do."

Even a concerted effort by the United States to wreck the Soviet economy through boycotts, embargoes, and a rising burden of military expenditure could scarcely have done as much damage as the policies and institutions of the Communist Party had wrought. But Reagan was certainly not helping matters. The military buildup over which he presided increased the pressure on Soviet planners. The Reagan Doctrine made the Soviet Union's outer empire appear less stable and more expensive than it had in the 1970s. Reagan's policies also affected the nonmilitary features of the correlation of forces in ways unfavorable to the Soviet Union. He managed to get American intermediate-range missiles deployed in Germany in the face of Soviet opposition, underscoring the basic solidarity of the Atlantic alliance. The American economic boom, even if it were not destined to last, and the drop in oil prices made the West stronger and the Eastern bloc weaker. The fall in the price of petroleum in fact cut Soviet hard currency earnings in half.

The resurgence of the West, coming in conjunction with the stagnation of the Soviet economy and the troubles of Soviet society, meant that the Soviet Union was falling farther behind the United States in the ongoing international competition between the two. Gorbachev's supreme task was to reverse this trend.

THE NEW REGIME

Soviet social and economic conditions claimed most of Gorbachev's attention once he became General Secretary. He demonstrated by what he did as well as by what he said that he believed the way to shore up his country's position beyond its borders was to improve its economic performance. There was not only an organic connection between Gorbachev's domestic and foreign policies, there were also marked similarities in the ways that he addressed the two sets of problems.

His domestic policies rested on the assumption that there was slack in the system, untapped potential for economic growth. Gorbachev and his colleagues believed they could do a great deal to raise morale and restore order through firm but limited measures. They counted on finding reserves that the old leadership had been too stodgy or too feeble to extract, and believed they could achieve significant results by mobilizing these reserves.

Adopting a more populist style than any that had been seen since Khrushchev's day, Gorbachev made a number of well-publicized personal appearances, both in Moscow and elsewhere, calling for openness in public life. Setting an example, he addressed the Soviet people more candidly, in speeches freer of the clichés of Communist optimism, than any of his recent predecessors. In May 1985 in Leningrad, for example, he delivered an unusually frank appraisal of the state of the Soviet economy. His aim was plainly to demonstrate that a new man was in charge and that a new era had begun.

He shook up the personnel at the top of the Soviet pyramid of authority. A series of promotions and retirements remade the Politburo as the old guard was eased out. Prime Minister Nikolai Tikhonov was retired. Viktor Grishin, the venerable Moscow Party chief, was pensioned off with neither thanks nor honors. Grigory Romanov, the Leningrad leader and Gorbachev's rival for the top position, lost his place in the ruling circle. Gromyko kept his seat on the Politburo but was kicked upstairs from the Foreign Ministry to the largely ceremonial position of President of the Supreme Soviet. A number of new faces appeared at the apex of the Party hierarchy. Six of the twelve members of the Politburo a year after Gorbachev took power had been added since his selection as General Secretary. The newcomers may not all have been Gorbachev's men—the second-in-command, Yegor Ligachev, was a potential rival—but they certainly were not Brezhnev's.

There was an actuarial inevitability to the turnover. Kosygin, Suslov, and Ustinov, as well as Chernenko, Andropov, and Brezhnev had died in office. Nonetheless, the infusion of new blood implied a particular attitude toward the problems of the Soviet Union and the measures necessary to address them. The turnover suggested that changing the personnel without changing the system itself would set things right in Russia. Every new man came from the ranks of that system. Several had earned reputations as disciplinarians and enforcers of orthodoxy. None was noted for his efforts to promote truly creative thinking or social, political or economic experimentation. Gorbachev was far from satisfied with the status quo, but he seemed to be saying that while the great Leninist-Stalinist machine needed a tuneup and new engineers in charge, it was not, fundamentally, broken and certainly not in need of replacement. Once the men who had been in charge were replaced, the economy would revive and the society would recover from the stagnation and despair of the late Brezhnev period.

Gorbachev and his associates did introduce some economic innovations, many of which had been broached during the brief Andropov interregnum. Teams of workers on collective farms, for instance, were given permission to keep or sell what they produced above a certain set level, rather than turning everything over to the state. This "brigade system" and other, similar measures, were familiar. They had long been discussed in authorized publications. They were hardly radical.

To spur the economy Gorbachev appeared intent on relying less on modest changes in the rules of production than on greater discipline, which Andropov had also emphasized. A campaign against alcoholism began. Police raided bars in search of truant workers. Mixed with the new disciplinary measures was another typically Soviet practice—exhortation. Gorbachev met with veterans of the Stakhanovite movement, named for the miner of the 1930s who was supposed to have vastly exceeded his quota of coal production. The new leader urged Soviet workers to follow Stakhanov's example. Slogans like "Don't just go to work: Work!" appeared everywhere.

These were not the policies of a leader who had made up his mind to venture beyond the boundaries of the familiar, the traditional and the politically safe. In a speech to East European Communists, Gorbachev was reported to have said that while they might be tempted to consider Western-style reforms as the salvation for their economies, they "should not think about life-savers but about the ship, and the ship is socialism." Like Russian leaders of the past, he wanted modernization but not democratization. He was an activist but not—at least by Western standards in his first eighteen months as leader—a reformer.

THE NEW LOOK

The same tactics and limits were evident in Gorbachev's foreign policy. There, too, his early initiatives reflected the belief that minor adjustments, cosmetic changes, and new forms of presentation would bring appreciable gains. He made several foreign trips. Even while Chernenko was alive, in December 1984, Gorbachev went to England to meet with Prime Minister Margaret Thatcher, Ronald Reagan's closest friend and staunchest supporter among the leaders of Western Europe. The Prime Minister was impressed. "I like Mr. Gorbachev," she said. "We can do business together."

In October 1985, before the November summit meeting, Gorbachev and his wife, Raisa, journeyed to Paris to meet with French President François Mitterrand. Mrs. Gorbachev made an impression as a stylish sophisticate. Not only did her wardrobe contrast with what earlier Kremlin first ladies had worn, but the very fact of her public appearances broke with the practice of Brezhnev's wife, who was seldom seen in public at all. In Andropov's case, it was not even known in the West whether or not he had a wife until she appeared at his funeral.

Gorbachev made himself more available to the Western press than any previous Soviet leader, even Khrushchev. He gave French journalists an interview before setting out for Paris and then conducted a press conference while there. He had recently given a lengthy interview to *Time* Magazine, responding both to written questions submitted in advance and to the queries of the magazine's editors in a two-hour session. He and Reagan videotaped brief New Year's messages that were broadcast on television in each other's countries on January 1, 1986.

At the November 1985 summit meeting, Gorbachev shared center stage for three days with his American counterpart. His participation in the meeting was a mark of his confidence in his own public skills. Indeed, it seems likely that one purpose of the summit from the Soviet point of view was to put these skills on worldwide display. Gorbachev also traveled within the Communist bloc. He marked the thirty-year extension of the Warsaw Pact by visiting the Polish capital in April 1985. He attended the Congress of the East German Communist Party in Berlin a year later. The message he aimed at foreign audiences was the same as the one intended for home consumption: A younger, more vigorous, more sophisticated leader had taken command in Moscow.

Gorbachev shuffled the personnel responsible for foreign as well as domestic policy. To replace Gromyko he chose Eduard Shevardnadze, the Party boss from the republic of Georgia and a man with no previous international experience. He brought Anatoly Dobrynin back to Moscow after twenty-five years as Ambassador in Washington to take charge of foreign affairs within the Central Committee Secretariat, the body through which the Communist Party exercises day-to-day supervision over the country's affairs, and moved several senior officials from the Foreign Ministry with experience in the West to the Secretariat to work for Dobrynin. One effect of these shifts was to put the Party's conduct of foreign policy in the hands of men much more knowledgeable than their predecessors about the world beyond Moscow and much better acquainted in particular with the United States, where several had been posted. Beginning in the latter part of 1985, some Western observers detected a more sophisticated tone to Soviet foreign policy and were inclined to credit it to Dobrynin and his associates.

Another effect of the changes was to give Gorbachev himself much tighter personal control over the Soviet Union's relations with other countries than his recent predecessors had maintained. During the first half of the 1980s, Soviet foreign policy had been largely in Gromyko's hands. For the second half of the decade, it was plain that the General Secretary intended to be his own foreign minister. As with domestic policy, there was also the implication that greater energy and fresh imagination would make it a more effective foreign policy.

Just as Gorbachev introduced some new policies in the management of the economy, so in foreign affairs the new regime hinted at departures from some of the patterns of the past. Soviet officials began telling their foreign contacts that the new leadership was seeking a way out of Afghanistan. In his speech to the Twenty-seventh Party Congress in February 1986, Gorbachev called the war there an "open wound." Reports of private meetings between Soviet and Israeli representatives suggested that diplomatic relations between the two countries, broken by the Soviets in the wake of the 1967 war, might be resumed; the two countries did hold low-level talks on consular representation, and the Soviet Foreign Minister met the Israeli Prime Minister at the United Nations in September 1986. This, in turn, opened the possibility of diplomatic progress in the Middle East as well as the prospect of further Jewish emigration from the Soviet Union. During the Soviet Party Congress Gorbachev permitted the Polish leader Wojciech Jaruzelski to pay a well-publicized visit to the city of Vilnius in the Soviet-controlled Baltic republic of Lithuania, a place of great sentimental and historical importance to the Polish people. The gesture was a clever way of bolstering the General's standing at home, which suffered from his close association with Moscow's policies. Moreover, Soviet representatives met with Chinese counterparts, and the official rhetoric in both Moscow and Beijing became distinctly more cordial. Elsewhere in East Asia, Shevardnadze paid a visit to Tokyo in January 1986, arousing speculation that Soviet-Japanese relations might be on the point of dramatic improvement.

THE LIMITS OF CHANGE

There were signs that the combination of minor policy adjustments, disciplinary measures and general encouragement that marked Gorbachev's first year as General Secretary did have an effect in both the domestic and foreign fields. The economic indicators turned modestly upward. The appearance of a vigorous man at the helm heartened cadres throughout the Soviet Union. Ordinary people, insofar as their feelings could be gauged, seemed to feel better about their government. They certainly entertained hopes for the future that Chernenko never inspired. In international relations, too, the new look made a difference. The personal contrast between Gorbachev and his predecessors left a favorable impression outside the Soviet Union. The new rhetoric and the hints of new initiatives heightened interest in Soviet foreign policy. American officials worried about the new challenge from Moscow.

Still, there were limits to what such changes could accomplish. There seemed to be some initial confusion in the conduct of foreign policy, perhaps because the people responsible were new to their jobs, perhaps because the new lines of responsibility were unclear, perhaps because the leader himself was inexperienced. On several occasions Moscow broadcast embarrassingly mixed signals to the rest of the world. While Gorbachev was in Berlin in April 1986 stressing the urgent need for arms-control negotiations with the United States, American planes attacked Libya in reprisal for the Libyan-sponsored bombing of a nightclub in Berlin that was frequented by American servicemen. Apparently feeling that they would lose face with their other clients by doing nothing in response to the American raid, the Soviets canceled the next scheduled meeting between Foreign Minister Shevardnadze and Secretary of State Shultz, which was to be devoted to planning for a second Reagan-Gorbachev summit meeting in 1986. They were thus sounding the alarm about the dangers of the arms race while refusing to take the steps necessary to restrain it. But if a summit did later take place, the Soviet outrage over Libya in April would seem, in retrospect, hollow and even cynical.

Similarly, in the midst of a public Soviet campaign for a complete ban on nuclear-weapon tests, the accident at the Chernobyl nuclear power plant occurred. Moscow's initial coverup of the disaster reinforced the Reagan Administration's warning that Soviet assurances on nuclear-arms testing and other matters could not be trusted.

Chernobyl might have been dismissed as one of those unforeseeable events that can happen to any country. Moscow recovered some of the lost ground in world opinion by belatedly providing a fairly full account and trying to link the accident with the dangers of nuclear weapons and Soviet proposals for addressing them. But the way was by no means open for sweeping Soviet gains in the international arena.

Six months previously, the Geneva summit had demonstrated the limits of purely personal diplomacy. While Gorbachev made a favorable impression on the watching world, he came away with nothing concrete. Reagan refused to budge in his commitment to strategic defense. The General Secretary returned home vulnerable to unfavorable comparison with his predecessor. While Brezhnev might not have been able to field questions from Western reporters as adeptly as Gorbachev did, at least he had obtained concessions on American military programs at his summit meetings with Nixon, Ford and Carter.

Even the new leader's attractive public manner was, potentially, a mixed blessing. While Gorbachev was impressive in delivering the political message that the Soviet leadership wished the world to hear, the message itself often had not changed much from the Brezhnev era. Asked by the French journalists about the conditions of Soviet Jews, he insisted that they enjoyed more political and human rights than Jews in any other country. It was a different assessment from the one offered, for example, by Anatoly Shcharansky, who came to the West a few months later after nine years in Soviet prisons and who enjoyed a higher reputation as an authority on the subject than the General Secretary.* Brezhnev would not have allowed himself to be interrogated by Western newsmen. The exposure that Gorbachev was willing to risk bespoke his self-confidence. In Brezhnev's day the official line on the Soviet treatment of Jews appeared in stilted, strident editorials in *Pravda* and *Izvestia*. But that line was not much different from the one which Gorbachev gave, and his spouting of the same old claims undercut the image he was trying to project as a new type of Soviet leader.

*Soviet Party leaders, even the most sophisticated of them, tend to have little exposure to the outside world. Gorbachev was no exception. It is possible that he actually did not fully understand the differences between the West and his own country in the protection of human rights. However, that ignorance would hardly make him a more attractive figure than if he had deliberately lied.

There was a disjunction between the medium and the message, a contrast between the modern man and the archaic, repressive policies he represented. The exiled Russian poet Joseph Brodsky has written of the supreme leader in a political system like that of the Soviet Union, "He had better be old, since old men never pretend that they are angels. The aging tyrant's sole purpose is to retain his position, and his demoguery and hypocrisy do not tax the minds of his subjects with the necessity of belief or textual proliferation. Whereas the young upstart with his true or false zeal and dedication always ends up raising the level of public cynicism."*

Although the wrapping in which his foreign policies were presented was new, the contents seemed familiar, at least before they could be examined and tested. Soviet interest in leaving Afghanistan, for instance, was not particularly novel. The Soviet authorities had not wanted to send troops in the first place. They had intervened reluctantly to keep a Soviet-sponsored regime in power. Gorbachev proposed to withdraw only if that goal were guaranteed. He was willing to stop fighting if the aim for which Soviet troops had fought for six years was achieved in some political-diplomatic settlement. This was logical enough from the Soviet point of view, but not particularly attractive to the West, let alone to the Afghans who were resisting the Soviet occupation.

Nothing really new materialized in Soviet policy toward the Middle East during Gorbachev's first year and a half. Moscow was embarrassed by Muamar Qadhafi's provocations and did nothing to assist him

*Joseph Brodsky, *Less Than One* (New York: Farrar, Straus and Giroux, 1986, p. 114).

when the United States struck back; but neither did the Soviet authorities disavow Qadhafi or pass up the opportunity to criticize the United States for retaliating. Contacts with Israel, such as they were, bore no immediate fruit; Soviet representatives walked out of the consular talks when the Israelis insisted on discussing Soviet Jews.

In Eastern Europe, Gorbachev seemed to be prepared to permit even less leeway than the ruling Communist Parties had enjoyed in the days of his predecessors. The local Communist leaders, in varying degrees, had charted cautiously independent courses in the 1980s. Hungary and East Germany especially had broadened their economic ties with the West. Although paying lip service to diversity within the bloc and acknowledging that each country "has its own specific interests, its own main problems," Gorbachev evidently wanted to reverse the trend toward diversity and independence and to integrate the Eastern bloc countries more closely with one another so as to force the Europeans to do more to help the Soviet economy. He insisted on renewing the Warsaw Treaty for thirty years, although some of the signatories wanted a shorter term.

To be sure, relations with China did improve. The two governments exchanged visits by high-ranking officials. The Soviet emissary was Deputy Prime Minister Ivan Arkhipov. They began to revive the economic and cultural programs that had fallen into abeyance with the Sino-Soviet split of the early 1960s.

However, that process of improvement predated Gorbachev's accession to power; it had been under way at least since 1982. Every Soviet leader since

Khrushchev has wished for improved relations with China. The initiative for the improvement in the 1980s came from the Chinese, who had their own reasons for it. On the one hand, they were less fearful of a Soviet attack than in the uneasy days of the late 1960s and early 1970s. On the other, they wanted to minimize the prospect of trouble on their borders so as to concentrate on economic modernization. Moreover, what improved was the relationship between the two governments. The Chinese and Soviet Communist Parties did not resume fraternal ties. The Soviets, in effect, conceded to the Chinese the right to interpret Communism in their own fashion. This was the same concession that Khrushchev had made to Tito of Yugoslavia in the 1950s and that Brezhnev felt he had to make to the Communist Parties of Western Europe in the 1970s. By moving to less acrimonious relations without insisting on ideological orthodoxy, Moscow was putting the interests of the Soviet state ahead of the cause of international Communism. But this was hardly a Gorbachev innovation. It was an old theme in the history of Soviet foreign policy, going back to the earliest days of the Soviet Union itself.

China had set three conditions for substantive, rather than merely token improvement in its relations with the Soviet Union: the withdrawal of Vietnamese troops from Cambodia; the evacuation of the Soviet Army from Afghanistan; and a reduction of Soviet forces on the Chinese border along with their total withdrawal from Mongolia. In his most interesting foreign policy speech as General Secretary, on July 28, 1986, in the Pacific port city of Vladivostok, Gorbachev made partial concessions on two of the Chinese demands. He announced that six Soviet regiments, totalling about 6,000 men, would be withdrawn from Afghanistan by the end of the year. He also proposed talks with the Chinese on force reductions. He suggested a regional security conference of all Pacific countries, along the lines of the Helsinki meeting of the European powers in 1975. But none of these measures by itself would have fundamentally changed the things to which the Chinese and others objected.

The speech embodied both the strengths and the shortcomings of the new Soviet foreign policy. In its tone and implications, it went beyond the tired, familiar, one-sided proposals. But in its concrete details and practical consequences, it did not go any appreciable distance in meeting the Chinese conditions. Nor did it address the most contentious issue between the Soviet Union and the East Asian country that, in economic terms, was much more important than China–Japan.

Indeed, Soviet-Japanese relations illustrate the basic problems of Soviet foreign policies and the limits of Gorbachev's approach to them. As one of the great economic powers of the world, Japan is a country of enormous potential importance for the Soviet Union. Because the two are neighbors and their economies complement one another, they could be economic partners on a large scale. Japan is poor in raw materials; Siberia and the Asian part of the Soviet Union are rich in them. The Soviets do not have the capital and technology to exploit them fully; Japan could supply both. Yet economic cooperation between the two has not flourished.

Political differences have stood in the way of a Soviet-Japanese economic partnership. The most important obstacle remains the Soviet occupation of the southern islands of the Kurile chain, which belonged to Japan until 1945. In August of that year, in the final days of the Pacific War, Stalin declared war on Japan and seized the islands. Since then the Soviet government has refused to give them up. To the contrary, it has progressively fortified them, with the most recent round of military construction and deployment coming in the 1980s.

No doubt the northern territories, as the Japanese call them, have some military value for the Soviet Union. But keeping them stands in the way of the enormous political and economic benefits that would come with better relations with Japan. Moscow could trade the islands for a great deal. There was no sign, however, that Gorbachev and his colleagues were considering such a trade. It posed the same dangers as economic reforms at home that would decentralize authority.

In both cases the Soviet leaders feared a ripple effect, a chain reaction. If they began to make concessions to other countries, they had to ask themselves, where would the process end? If the Soviets gave back the northern territories, they could expect the Chinese to press all the harder their claims for territories along the border between the two countries that they said the czars had stolen in the nineteenth century. The Eastern Europeans and the Baltic peoples, perhaps even the Armenians and the Ukrainians, not to mention the Muslims of Soviet Central Asia, would not be far behind. The United States could return Okinawa to Japan without worrying that the Federal Republic of Germany would leave NATO or that Hawaii or Kansas would be moved to seek independence. But the Soviet empire and the Soviet Union itself are fragile in a way that the West is not. They are held together by force, not consent.

Abroad as well as at home, therefore, the Soviet leaders were haunted by the fear that if they opened the door to reform a crack, they would let in a flood of changes that would sweep them away. These fears were not groundless. As a dedicated son of the Party, Gorbachev was unlikely to be free from them. In foreign policy, as in economic and social affairs, he was energetic but orthodox.

The postwar period offers a precedent for more substantial changes of direction in Soviet relations with the rest of the world than any the Gorbachev regime produced in its first eighteen months. In the two years after the death of Stalin in 1953, the men who succeeded him took a series of steps that could serve as a standard of comparison for the Gorbachev foreign policy. The circumstances in 1985 were not precisely what they had been in 1953, but they were not wholly dissimilar. In both cases a whole chapter of Soviet history, an era, had come to an end. A long agenda of unfinished business awaited the successors in each case. To be sure, the end of Stalin's regime was traumatic for the Soviet Union in a way that the passing of the Brezhnev generation was not, and the Soviet Union was a much more powerful presence in the world in 1985 than it was in 1953 and so perhaps less inclined to be tractable in its foreign policy. On the other hand, the leadership was more collective in 1953 than in 1985. Although Gorbachev is not an entirely free agent, he probably enjoys more flexibility, at least in foreign policy, than was available to the triumvirate of Georgi Malenkov, Nikolai Bulganin and Khrushchev thirty-odd years before.

The post-Stalin leadership renounced the teaching, handed down from Marx to Lenin to Stalin himself, that war between the capitalist and communist camps is inevitable. The Soviet Union officially recognized that nuclear weapons had changed the world. "The atomic bomb," said one official pronouncement, "does not conform to the class principle." The new leadership also reconciled itself with Tito, who had broken with Stalin in 1948. In 1953 the Soviet Union used its influence on North Korea to help bring an end to the Korean War. In 1955 the Soviets concluded the Austrian State Treaty, withdrawing troops from their zone of occupation in that country, which then became fully independent and neutral but essentially a member of the Western community of nations. They also gave up bases in Hanko in Finland and in Port Arthur, Manchuria, both of which Stalin had taken after the war. The new leadership even sent out feelers to the West about the reunification and neutralization of Germany that seem more serious in retrospect than they were considered by Western authorities at the time.

Leadership successions offer opportunities for changes of policy in the Soviet Union. Gorbachev came to office recognizing, indeed proclaiming, the need for change. But even by the standards of Soviet history, specifically by the precedent of the post-Stalin transition, and even within the boundaries available to an orthodox Soviet leader, the changes he initially introduced were modest.

It is possible that Gorbachev's freedom of action on Afghanistan, the Middle East, and East Asia was limited by a delicate balance of power within the leadership during his first year in office. Or he may have judged the policies that he inherited to be, on the whole, satisfactory. Or he may simply have decided to put to one side anything that did not directly concern relations with the United States. It was clear that Soviet-American relations had the highest priority for the new leadership. After Gorbachev came to power, Soviet officials as well as some Western observers suggested that he was shifting the center of attention of Soviet foreign policy from the United States to other countries. In April 1986 Aleksandr Yakovlev, the new chief of propaganda in the Party Secretariat, wrote an article saying that "the Soviet Union decisively repudiates the model of so-called 'bipolarity' and the distorted conception of two 'superpowers'. . . . The USSR is significantly activating its relations with capitalist countries other than the U.S., with their regional groupings and organizations." Even the General Secretary himself hinted at such a shift. "We live in a single house," he told French journalists before his visit to Paris, "although some of us come into the house by one entrance and others through another entrance. We need to cooperate and lay down communications in this house."

Gorbachev did pay special attention to Western Europe. Besides traveling to Britain and France, he visited East Berlin, the Eastern bloc's window on the West and the Communist-controlled city in which he would attract the widest attention throughout Europe. The rest of the world had not, however, supplanted the United States as the focus of Soviet foreign policy, despite the claims of some Soviet spokesmen and the theories of some Western analysts. The quarter-century Washington career of Anatoly Dobrynin did not qualify him as a French or Japanese specialist, yet he was summoned to sit at Gorbachev's right hand in the inner sanctum of power.

Shifting priorities away from U.S.-Soviet relations would have made little sense. For one thing, the fundamental disputes between the Soviet Union and these other countries were in some ways more serious than its differences with the United States and therefore less amenable to diplomatic accommodation. Americans disliked the Soviet political system and ideology. To the Germans, the Japanese, and the Chinese, the Soviet Union was, in one way or another, actually occupying their territory.

In courting these "middle powers," especially the Europeans, Moscow was pursuing an old and hallowed tactic. It was trying to put pressure indirectly on Washington. It was hoping that the Europeans would lobby the Reagan Administration on behalf of measures that the Kremlin favored. Gorbachev was simply the latest and perhaps the most articulate Soviet spokesman to try to go over the heads of Western leaders to Western public opinion and political elites. The appeal to "progressive" elements in the West has been a staple of Soviet policy since the revolution.

The United States had first place on the Soviet foreign policy agenda for another, more powerful reason. It was the United States, and the United States alone, that controlled the world's other great nuclear arsenal. The United States could destroy all that Communism had built in Russia. The United States was central to the Soviet Union for the same reason that the Soviet Union was central to the United

States. Ultimately, it was the imperative of regulating their nuclear rivalry that brought the leaders of the two countries to the summit.

The nuclear relationship was always a matter of more than casual interest to the Soviet leadership. Reagan's policies had made it more urgent than usual. Here, too, the American President was trying to diminish, even liquidate a Soviet achievement, indeed the most important achievement of the Brezhnev generation—nuclear parity. At the heart of Soviet concern about the nuclear balance was the greatest, the most controversial, and potentially the most revolutionary innovation of Reagan's presidency, the Strategic Defense Initiative.

4

THE GOD FROM
THE MACHINE

While Gorbachev criticized what he saw as the failures and shortcomings of the Brezhnev era, he was also determined to protect and consolidate its principal achievement, the creation of a strategic nuclear arsenal that in many respects matched, and in some exceeded, the capability of American forces.

It is almost solely by virtue of its military power that the Soviet Union qualifies as a superpower at all, and its nuclear weaponry is the ultimate manifestation of that power. Theoreticians can debate whether, and in what sense, nuclear arms are useful—that is, whether they can be used against enemy targets to achieve military advantage; but there is little question that they are meaningful. They matter a great deal, even if they are never detonated. They cast a shadow over the geopolitical terrain where the United States and the Soviet Union compete for influence and clients. During the 1970s, the shadow cast by the nuclear arsenal of the U.S.S.R. grew longer and more ominous.

The Soviets were determined to match the United States in nuclear weaponry no matter what the cost, but the cost was not all that great. Nuclear weapons are at once extraordinarily powerful and comparatively cheap. A single one can incinerate a large city. It is well within the means of a modern industrial country to have many. The United States and the Soviet Union acquired thousands without putting undue strain on their economies.

In addition to safeguarding the Motherland from foreign attack, the Kremlin's nuclear arsenal guaranteed its empire in Europe. The Soviet Union could send troops to crush rebellions there without fear that the West, no matter how sympathetic to the rebels, would intervene. By the time Gorbachev became General Secretary, Soviet diplomats, soldiers, propagandists and KGB operatives in the Third World could go about their business more confidently and assertively, knowing that they were backed by the formidable firepower of the Strategic Rocket Forces. The United States was less likely to challenge the Soviet Union as long as there was a risk of armed conflict and escalation to nuclear war. In that sense, from the standpoint of the Kremlin, Soviet nuclear power was a deterrent that made the world safer than it would otherwise be for Soviet expansionism. Thus, there was a direct link between the Soviets' acquisition in the 1970s of new footholds in the Third World and the buildup, in the same period, of their strategic arsenal.

But by the time Gorbachev became General Secretary, something had changed profoundly on the American side. The United States under Ronald Reagan seemed bent on repudiating precisely the status quo that Gorbachev was at once so conscious of having inherited and so determined to protect. Just as the instrument for reversing the geopolitical advances of Moscow's expansionist heyday was the Reagan Doctrine, so the American instrument for nullifying the benefits of the Soviet nuclear-weapons buildup was the Strategic Defense Initiative (SDI). The Reagan Doctrine evolved in fits and starts during the first term, replacing the President's earlier rhetorical emphasis on the rollback of Communism inside the East bloc. SDI came out of the blue. For the first years of the Reagan presidency, the Administration stressed its "strategic modernization" program of 1981, a large, expensive buildup in offensive weaponry consisting mostly of programs started before Reagan took office. When the President unveiled SDI in March 1983, it seemed unlikely to replace the strategic modernization program as the Administration's driving preoccupation. Yet by the second term that is exactly what happened.

SDI was the single most contentious issue on the agenda of arms control. Arms control, in turn, was the single most enduring piece of business that engaged the superpowers.

The intractability of other issues made all but impossible anything more than occasional agreements-to-disagree in areas such as regional competition and human rights. The United States could complain about the way the Soviet regime treated its own people or those of nations it dominated; Washington might even sometimes extract concessions in the form of increased Jewish emigration or the release of an occasional dissident. But by granting these concessions, the Kremlin was making tactical exceptions to its long-standing insistence on non-interference in the internal affairs of the U.S.S.R. In the final analysis, what the Soviet leaders were most determined to protect against Western influence was the Soviet internal order, since that was the soil in which their own personal power was rooted. As for regional competition, regardless of declarations they might sign, either at the Moscow summit in 1972 or anywhere else, each side was bent on seeking "unilateral advantage" over the other. Two such large, powerful and ambitious nations could hardly avoid bumping up against each other globally, and given their different values and interests, their interaction could only be competitive.

The Soviet-American relationship was marked by such irreconcilable hostility and profound mistrust that it defied systematic accommodation in all areas except one—the joint regulation of the military competition. The composition of their arsenals of last resort was virtually the only subject on which the superpowers could negotiate in anything approaching a profitable and protracted way.

That feature of the relationship is less paradoxical than it might sound. The Soviet Union and the United States are adversaries because of the political differences between them; their military rivalry is the outward manifestation of the essentially political conflict. Moreover, nuclear weapons are so powerful and so unpredictable that the two sides not only frighten and deter each other, they also frighten and deter themselves. It is often said that the United States and the Soviet Union would have gone to war against each other since the end of World War II had it not been for the existence of nuclear weapons. Instead of using these weapons to fight, the two countries have used them to maneuver for political advantage and, at the same time, to diminish the danger of catastrophic military conflict. This peculiar exercise in sublimation—this turning of Clausewitz's famous maxim on its head, so that politics becomes the conduct of war by other means—is what arms control is all about: a joint effort to enforce the military peace while simultaneously conducting the political contest.

During the 1970s, arms control became a firmly established part of the form and substance of Soviet-American relations, institutionalized in the bureaucracies of both sides. Despite objections from right and left in the United States, arms control became the centerpiece of Soviet-American relations in general and of summitry in particular. It survived shock waves emitted by disruptive events in other areas of the competition; it survived the misgivings of laymen and experts alike about Soviet compliance; it survived the vacillations of American public opinion; it survived the persistent temptation of politicians to impose "linkage" between the specific enterprise of arms control and the general climate of the relationship.

The Reagan Administration posed the ultimate test of arms control and its staying power. The President and some of his top officials at first had no use at all for arms control, made no bones about their hostility to the enterprise, and, when forced for reasons of political expediency to go through the motions of negotiating, made proposals that were so far from being acceptable to the Soviet side as to seem designed to prevent an agreement. In its first term the Administration made a series of what were intended by some members of the government, if not the President himself, to be "killer" proposals designed to prevent agreements.* Yet, once again, the enterprise survived. Old agreements, although fraying at the edges, remained in force, and negotiations toward new agreements continued, although with more breakdowns than breakthroughs.

SDI had ambiguous implications for the resilient yet problematic core of the Soviet-American relationship. It might do what Soviet invasions, conservative congressmen, hawkish lobbying groups and other forces unfriendly to arms control had failed to accomplish—end the negotiations once and for all. Or it might, to the contrary, do what patient negotiators and summiteers had failed to achieve—provide the catalyst for a new kind of arms control that would not only regulate the military competition, but also reverse the quantitative buildup and inhibit qualitative changes in weaponry.

Therefore, of all the issues that divided Reagan and Gorbachev—and of all the issues that they discussed at the first summit in 1985—SDI was the most important. In the wake of that meeting, it became, if anything, even more important. Other arms-control issues, particularly those of intermediate-range nuclear forces (INF) and confidence-building measures to reduce the danger of a war starting by inadvertence, seemed more susceptible to agreement. But that was largely because those issues did not lie at the core of the strategic relationship and the arrangement whereby the superpowers kept the nuclear peace. It

*This thesis is elaborated by Strobe Talbott in *Deadly Gambits: The Reagan Administration and the Stalemate in Nuclear Arms Control* (New York: Alfred A. Knopf, 1984, and Vintage Books, 1985).

was a troubled core, indeed a troubled relationship and a precarious arrangement. SDI was both a cause and an effect of those troubles.

BUSINESS AS USUAL

Nuclear weapons are so vastly cost-efficient, offering so much bang for the buck, that they defy any known defense. Only a few weapons have to penetrate enemy defenses to do immense damage. When one side has discovered a way to protect itself even partially against the delivery system of the other, it has soon found itself faced with a new delivery system.

Before the era of détente, each side undertook strenuous efforts first to avoid, and later to reverse, the consequences of the growth of the other's nuclear arsenal. Even as each nation built weapons that increased the vulnerability of the other, each sought to make itself *in*vulnerable. In the 1950s and 1960s the superpowers pursued offense and defense simultaneously. First they threatened each other with bombers and defended themselves with anti-aircraft installations. But air defenses only stimulated the development of an offensive countermeasure, the intercontinental ballistic missile (ICBM), which is able to fly high above jet fighters and surface-to-air missiles. Later came another countermeasure, the cruise missile, which can fly below and avoid tracking by enemy anti-aircraft radar. In the 1960s both sides developed anti-ballistic missiles (ABMs), but they soon learned that these could be overwhelmed with multiple independently targetable re-entry vehicles, or

MIRVs. Indeed, the United States pioneered the development of MIRVs in part as a countermeasure to the ABM system that the Soviets erected around Moscow.

Eventually the leaders of the two countries decided that it was futile to try to shield themselves against nuclear missiles. This realization was adopted as policy on the American side first. That occurred after a debate within the U.S. government that anticipated, in a number of respects, the controversy over SDI. In December 1966, President Lyndon Johnson met in Austin, Texas, with his principal military advisers—Secretary of Defense Robert McNamara, his deputy Cyrus Vance, the presidential national security adviser Walt Rostow, and the Joint Chiefs of Staff. The session turned into a heated dispute over whether the Executive Branch should request funds from Congress to produce an American ABM system comparable to the one the Soviets were already putting in place. The five chiefs, with Rostow's backing, favored such a budget request, while McNamara and Vance opposed it. McNamara has recalled his argument:

> The proper response to a Soviet ABM system is not the deployment of an admittedly "leaky" U.S. defense. The proper response is action which will ensure that we maintain our deterrent capability in the face of Soviet defense. . . .If our deterrent force was of the proper size before the Soviets deployed their defenses, it must now be expanded to ensure that the same number of weapons will land on Soviet targets, after taking account of the attrition the U.S. missile force will suffer as they pass through the Soviet defenses. So for the United States to deploy an

ABM defense is the wrong response to the Soviet action. But since we are in this bind, why don't we do this: put a small amount of money in the budget for ABM procurement, but state in the budget, and in my written report to the Congress, that none of those funds will be spent, and no decision will be made to deploy an ABM system, until after we make every possible effort to negotiate an agreement with the Soviets which will prohibit deployment of defenses by either side and will limit offensive forces as well.

A leak-proof defense was impossible; the less expensive, more sensible way to counter defense was with additional offense; and the prospect of an American defense should be used as leverage, or a bargaining chip, in arms control. That view prevailed. At a summit meeting in Glassboro, New Jersey, in 1967, Johnson and McNamara began the process of convincing a skeptical Soviet premier, Aleksei Kosygin, of the perverse but, as they saw it, compelling logic of mutual vulnerability. "Mr. Prime Minister," said McNamara, "deployment of a Soviet ABM system will lead to an escalation of the arms race. That's not good for either one of us."

As McNamara recalled the occasion, Kosygin grew agitated. His face turned red and he pounded on the table, exclaiming, "Defense is moral; offense is immoral!"*

Ultimately, however, the Soviets came to agree with the Americans. They did so in the course of the Strategic Arms Limitation Talks (SALT). In 1972 Richard Nixon and Leonid Brezhnev signed the SALT I treaty, which strictly limited the ABMs of

*Robert McNamara, *Blundering Into Disaster: Surviving the First Century of the Nuclear Age* (New York: Pantheon, 1986).

both sides. In signing the ABM treaty, the superpowers recognized that the defensive technology then available could not neutralize the dirty little secret of nuclear weaponry: its extraordinary cost-effectiveness. To that extent, it was a highly practical rather than philosophical measure; by banning large-scale, nationwide defenses, the treaty made a virtue out of a necessity, given the inability of such defenses to cope with offensive countermeasures. But there was also, embedded in the treaty, an open-ended recognition that deterrence depended on the mutual vulnerability of the two societies. For that reason, in addition to limiting defenses based on technologies then available, the treaty also placed restrictions on the development and testing of those that might become available in the future; and the pact was to be of unlimited duration.

SALT also amounted to an understanding that if defense was to be constrained, offense must be as well. In 1972, in addition to the ABM treaty, there was an interim agreement on offensive weapons, followed seven years later by the SALT II treaty. While these pacts did impose some quantitative and qualitative rules on the arms race, the competition in offensive weapons, and in permissible ABM research and development, continued vigorously. The way in which the Soviets ran their part of the race raised doubts in the United States about whether the Kremlin truly accepted the assumptions underlying the ABM treaty.

The United States and the Soviet Union are marked by many differences in their geographical situations, historical experience, alliance obligations, adversary relationships, and areas of technological and industrial strength and weakness. Russia has traditionally been a land power whose military has greatly valued artillery; the United States has, since its birth, been a maritime nation and early in this century became an air power as well. Those basic differences in military tradition are reflected in the composition of the two sides' arsenals of last resort: the Soviets have given priority to land-based ballistic missiles, the artillery of the nuclear age, while the United States has diversified its strategic forces on land, at sea and in the air.

This difference in the mix of forces has complicated attempts to gauge parity and to codify it through the various agreements reached in SALT in the 1970s. Because of their heavy reliance on land-based missiles and because their missiles have tended to be behemoths that make up in lifting power what they lack in sophisticated, miniaturized propulsion, guidance and explosives, the Soviets have developed over the years a preponderance in one kind of nuclear weapon: ICBMs and their warheads, or MIRVs.

Land-based ballistic missiles equipped with multiple warheads have certain characteristics that make them especially threatening: they are fast, accurate and highly destructive. Since they are based on land, they are all in a constant state of high alert, readily controlled by political authorities, and subject to launch at a moment's notice.

For some years, there had been growing concern expressed outside the government—and echoed inside—that the asymmetries in ICBM warheads and the capacity to hurl them ("ballistic missile throw-weight") were the ones that really mattered. These were asymmetries that could not be adequately offset because ICBM warheads were the potential or theoretical instruments of a Soviet first strike against "hard targets" in the United States—concrete-protected, underground silos housing American ICBMs. The supposedly compensating American lead in bombers, cruise missiles and SLBMs was of little comfort since those were weapons suitable only for a second, retaliatory strike. Bombers and cruise missiles were too slow to carry out a sneak attack, and SLBMs (submarine-launched missiles) were too imprecise to destroy enemy ICBM silos. Only ICBM warheads qualified, in the jargon, as "prompt hard-target killers" that could strike the enemy's missiles swiftly and accurately enough to destroy them in their silos. In the games of chicken that the superpowers played, or were presumed prepared to play, many thought it was hard-target killers that counted most. The U.S.S.R. could, according to these calculations, threaten American ICBM silos with preemptive attack; the United States could not do the same in reverse. There was, in short, a critical asymmetry in vulnerabilities.

With the Soviet Union's excess of prompt hard-target kill capability, and with many additional weapons in reserve on other delivery vehicles, the day might come when the Kremlin could blind American command-and-control facilities, wipe out the entire force of 1,000 American ICBM silos, and destroy many bombers before they could take off and submarines before they could put to sea. With the loss of its ICBMs, the United States would be unable to attack the most valuable Soviet military targets; any American bombers and submarines that escaped initial destruction would only be able to take haphazard vengeance on Soviet cities. Yet the Soviets would still have sufficient weapons remaining for a second attack on American cities if such a retaliation were attempted. Hence the United States might surrender without firing a shot. Even if no Kremlin leadership would actually risk launching such an attack, the Soviets' perceived ability to do so might give them a decisive psychological edge in a showdown with the United States over Central Europe, the oil fields of the Persian Gulf, or some other strategically vital Third World trouble spot.

But would any imaginable Soviet leadership indulge in such a grotesque gamble with the lives of its own people and those of all other countries? It was in answer to that question, which had been asked for some time, that a second complaint about the nuclear status quo emerged during the 1970s: the Soviet Union was precisely the one superpower that might actually start a nuclear war; therefore it was especially imprudent to grant it the theoretical capacity to do so.

In the many debates during the 1970s about the strategic balance, a Soviet nuclear attack against the United States was taken seriously not only because of the nature of the Soviet arsenal but also because of the nature of the Soviet Union. Even the champions of détente and the defenders of SALT admitted in their arguments with the hawks that they could well imagine a Kremlin leader who would attack the United States if he felt he could, in some sense, get away with it. An American nuclear attack against the U.S.S.R. was not taken as seriously simply because Americans did not perceive their own country to be that sort of superpower.*

Thus one of the most important gaps between the superpowers is at once the most obvious, in other ways the most easily and frequently omitted from analysis and discourse: an aggressiveness or malevolence gap that Americans naturally see favoring the U.S.S.R. in time of war or even in time of political crisis. That gap has magnified the importance of all others, particularly the perennially troublesome one in prompt hard-target kill capability, which grew during the 1970s and which seemed to fortify both the objective and subjective arguments against SALT, détente and parity.

Reagan took these gaps seriously. During his 1980 presidential campaign and well into his first term, he declared repeatedly that the Soviet Union enjoyed net military supremacy over the United States. He was by no means the first candidate to accuse his predecessor of having allowed the United States to slip onto the wrong side of a nuclear-weapons gap,

---

*There is a contradiction between Americans' image of themselves and what their government has felt it necessary to say in public about its intentions: the United States' long-standing official, publicly declared policy of providing a "nuclear umbrella" for its allies depends explicitly on keeping open the option of initiating the use of nuclear weapons in retaliation for a *conventional*—that is, non-nuclear—Soviet attack on Western Europe. The Soviet Union, having no far-flung allies to whom it needs to provide the benefits of "extended deterrence," has been able to engage in the doctrinal and propagandistic luxury of eschewing the option of first use of nuclear weapons and taunting the United States for its refusal of a joint renunciation of first use.

but he was the first President who, once in office, continued to assert that the gap existed.* In March 1982 Reagan said at a news conference, "The truth of the matter is that on balance the Soviet Union does have a definite margin of superiority." He and other officials spoke repeatedly of "the window of vulnerability" not as a hypothetical danger the United States would face if certain unfavorable trends continued, but as an actual condition. This, Reagan argued, was solely an *American* vulnerability, not the mutual vulnerability that was believed to hold the key to deterrence.

The Joint Chiefs of Staff were, understandably, uncomfortable with the contention that their forces were inferior to the enemy's. They found it difficult to accept the idea that the theoretical vulnerability of one-third of the American deterrent constituted a net disadvantage, especially since, according to the logic underlying the concern about the window of vulnerability, *two*-thirds of the Soviet deterrent would be theoretically vulnerable (land-based missiles in fixed-site silos) if the United States acquired sufficient hard-target kill capability of its own. Not only did the Chiefs still hold that parity between the superpowers existed, but they believed in the SALT II treaty of 1979. They calculated that in the absence of the trea-

*In the 1950s there was considerable concern among American military experts that the Soviets had acquired enough intercontinental bombers to attack the bases of the Strategic Air Command, depriving the United States of its ability to retaliate. The fear of American vulnerability to a disarming first strike increased considerably as the Soviets began testing intercontinental-range missiles. The alleged existence of a "missile gap" was played up by John Kennedy in his campaign against Richard Nixon.

ty's limits on land-based MIRVs, the Soviets could increase the threat posed by the U.S.S.R.'s Strategic Rocket Forces considerably faster and more cheaply than the United States could take countermeasures. It was because of this stand by the Chiefs that the Administration adopted the curious policy that the United States would invite the Soviets to join in an informal, open-ended arrangement of "not undercutting" SALT II, even though Reagan had denounced it as "fatally flawed" and even though the Senate had never ratified it.

Reagan was never comfortable with even this concession to the old regime (of which the Chiefs were a holdover, since they had been appointed by Carter). The Reagan Administration went through more than five years of private bickering and public ambivalence over whether to honor SALT. Part of the reason that the President was never at ease even with the "no-undercut" policy on SALT was his conviction that the Soviets themselves were constantly undercutting the treaties.

The Soviets proved shameless at chiseling on the margins of the agreements and adept at justifying what they had done. In many instances they took advantage of imprecisions and loopholes in the agreements. In two cases—one involving a large radar facility in Siberia, the other a mobile, single-warhead ICBM they were developing in addition to a new ICBM carrying multiple warheads that they were allowed by SALT II—they seemed to have crossed the boundary not just of the spirit but of the letter of the agreements. The most charitable interpretation was that in order to be in strict compliance with the treaty, the Soviets would have had to locate their early-warning radar in the remote tundra; they had decided to save money by locating it instead where it was cheaper to build, even though the location technically violated the treaty. The more sinister explanation was that the Siberian radar was intended as part of a potential nationwide ABM network of the sort proscribed by SALT I. But even as Washington protested the radar, the President was launching SDI, a program explicitly dedicated to the goal of an ABM system far more comprehensive and sophisticated than anything the Soviets seemed to have in mind.

As for the Soviets' new, mobile ICBM, the United States complained that it was a "second new type" of ICBM and therefore not permitted under SALT II, which provided for the deployment of only one new type. The Soviet claim that it was merely an updated version of an old missile rested on certain idiosyncracies in the SALT II treaty that came about largely as a result of the Pentagon's desire, during the Carter Administration, to preserve options for new missiles of its own. The Soviet missile in question was roughly the counterpart to the "Midgetman" ICBM that was strongly advocated by a bipartisan coalition of members of Congress and a presidential commission of outside experts chaired by Brent Scowcroft, a retired Air Force general who had served as President Ford's national security adviser. After the new U.S. ten-warhead ICBM (or MX), the Midgetman would, when fully developed, have been a second American "new type."

In response to a barrage of American charges that they failed to honor their obligations under SALT I, the Soviets argued that the United States' refusal to ratify SALT II kept the world in a state of anxiety over how much longer America would abide by the treaty, if only informally. In 1986 the latest round of the ongoing bureaucratic squabble between the Departments of State and Defense was resolved in a compromise under which the United States would remain in technical compliance with one SALT II ceiling, because doing so was militarily and financially expedient, but would exceed another ceiling later in the year because otherwise it might have slightly impinged on the Reagan buildup.

Political pressures both from the West European allies and from Congress made it impossible simply to let arms control lapse, as many in the Reagan Administration would have preferred. Whatever the public disappointment with the record of the détente era, there was still strong support for arms control. No President, not even one as popular as Reagan, could afford to appear to be walking away from the negotiating table. Thus in addition to observing the arms-control treaties already concluded, albeit grudgingly, Reagan began negotiations for a new one. Early in his presidency, he attempted to negotiate *toward* a position of superiority and to establish a margin of safety for the United States by means of arms control. He said he was in favor of "real arms control" that would achieve reductions in nuclear weapons rather than the mere limitations of the SALT II. The failure of SALT II to effect reductions was, he said in June 1986 (in the same press conference at which he explained his decision to break with the treaty later in the year), his principal objection to it:

> The treaty was really nothing but the legitimizing of an arms race. It didn't do anything to reduce nuclear weapons or the nuclear threat. All it did was regulate

how fast and how much we could continue increasing the number of weapons. So I was always hostile to that particular treaty because it did not reduce weapons.

The "L" in SALT stood for limitation. When, in 1982, Reagan had embarked on his own attempt to improve on SALT, he bestowed on a new negotiation the acronym START, for Strategic Arms *Reduction* Talks. He made a proposal that called for very dramatic reductions indeed—primarily in the arsenal of the Soviet Union. He proposed that the Soviet Union reduce its ICBM warheads by 60 percent. There was to be virtually no tradeoff in the existing American arsenal for this major Soviet concession. The United States would have had to pay a price in the number of future weapons it could deploy, but it would not have had to give up any of the existing programs in its strategic modernization program. It would have been permitted to proceed with the development and deployment of the MX; a new SLBM with hard-target kill capability, the Trident II; two new bombers designed to penetrate Soviet air defenses, the B-1 and the Advanced-Technology Bomber (ATB), or "Stealth," which would be nearly invisible to enemy radar; and a family of new cruise missiles.

The President's formula was simple enough: he was asking the Soviets to build down while the United States built up. In his obsession with achieving reductions, however, he was adopting a prescription that would actually exacerbate the theoretical vulnerability of the American ICBM force. In addition to seeking deep cuts in warheads, his proposal included such low limits on launchers (ICBM silos, submarine launching tubes and intercontinental bombers) that the resulting ratio of Soviet warheads to American ICBM silos would *increase*. This unintended irony in the U.S. START position caused muted consternation among members of the Administration. It was like Woody Allen's joke in the movie *Annie Hall*, about two women in a restaurant: One says, "The food here is terrible," and the other replies, "Yes, and the portions are so small." The Soviets would not agree to what the United States was proposing—and the United States would, arguably, be worse off if they did.

These thrusts and parries were nothing more than nuclear business as usual. All of the deployments, proposals, and campaigns were based on the assumption that offensive weapons would remain the instruments of deterrence and that the 1972 accord limiting defense would remain in force. None of these moves changed the bedrock condition of the nuclear age, the mutual vulnerability of the two societies.

THE POWER OF AN IDEA

The President was scheduled to give a television speech on March 23, 1983, primarily to rally support for a new American ICBM, the MX. It was what his aides and speechwriters referred to as "the standard threat speech." This particular version was nicknamed "MX-plus"—"plus" because of its surprise ending. At the end of the speech Reagan unexpectedly added this passage:

> Wouldn't it be better to save lives than to avenge them?. . .After careful consultation with my advisors, including the Joint Chiefs of Staff, I believe

there is a way. Let me share with you a vision of the future which offers hope. It is that we embark on a program to counter the awesome Soviet missile threat with measures that are defensive. . .What if free people could live secure in the knowledge that their security did not rest upon the threat of instant U.S. retaliation to deter a Soviet attack, that we could intercept and destroy strategic ballistic missiles before they reached our own soil or that of our allies?. . .I call upon the scientific community in our country, those who gave us nuclear weapons, to turn their great talents now to the cause of mankind and world peace, to give us the means of rendering these nuclear weapons impotent and obsolete.

What Reagan was proposing was nothing short of a revolution in the nuclear order. If what he called for could be achieved, it would be as revolutionary a change in international politics and Soviet-American relations as the invention of the bomb itself. This was not a proposal to solve the strategic problem that had preoccupied his three predecessors, the supposed vulnerability of American land-based missiles. It was, rather, a way of altering the strategic landscape so drastically that the problem would cease to exist. Offensive weapons themselves would no longer matter. The defenses the President sought would repudiate the basic premise of the nuclear age, on which all the nuclear-weapons policies of both superpowers had been based: the unchallengeable superiority of offense. It would replace vulnerability with invulnerability. Technology, in the Reagan vision of the future, would overwhelm and reshape politics.

For anyone with a memory for old films, the President's speech announcing SDI might have seemed an instance of life imitating art. In 1940 Reagan starred in a Warner Brothers spy picture, *Murder in the Air*. He played Brass Bancroft, a double agent who is assigned to help protect a vital U.S. military secret, the "Inertia Projector," an airborne death-ray that could destroy enemy aircraft before they could bomb the United States This "new super-weapon," according to the film,

> not only makes the United States invincible in war, but in so doing promises to become the greatest force for world peace ever discovered, which is the hope and prayer of all thinking people, regardless of race, creed or government.

Twenty-six years later, in 1966, Alfred Hitchcock made an espionage thriller called *Torn Curtain*. In the film, the Pentagon is trying to develop a system of "anti-missile missiles." But first the Americans must get their hands on a complex formula known only to an East German scientist. So a physicist with the all-American name Michael Armstrong, played by the all-American actor Paul Newman, pretends to defect to East Germany. He arrives in East Berlin and gives a press conference, at which he explains the purpose of his mission: "We will produce a defensive weapon that will make all offensive nuclear weapons obsolete, and thereby abolish the terror of nuclear warfare."

Reagan, who frequently drew from the movies in his own press conferences and speeches, may have remembered some combination of those dramatic bits of monologue from *Murder in the Air* and *Torn Curtain* and used it for the punch line of his March 23, 1983, speech. In any event, the idea for what became known as "Star Wars" had been germinating in his mind for some time. When his political horizons had begun to expand from the state of California, he naturally thought about the responsibilities of the Oval Office. As early as 1976, when he was challenging Gerald Ford for the Republican nomination, he criticized deterrence, comparing the arrangement to two people with guns cocked at each other's head. In 1979 he toured the headquarters of the North American Air Defense (NORAD) Command deep inside Cheyenne Mountain in Colorado. He asked the NORAD commander-in-chief a question: What could the United States do if its radar spotted a Soviet missile coming? He received a straightforward answer: nothing. The United States survived from day to day on the sufferance of the Soviet Union; the day that the Politburo decided otherwise, there was nothing the United States could do about it other than retaliate and incinerate millions of Russians. "Gee," he commented after listening to a national-security expert, "it's a helluva way to run a railroad, isn't it?"

At Reagan's behest, one of his advisers, Martin Anderson, later wrote a memorandum urging consideration of a program to replace the ABM treaty with a protective anti-missile system. Such a thing, said the memo, "is probably fundamentally far more appealing to the American people than the questionable satisfaction of knowing that those who initiated an attack against us were also blown away."

Left to his own devices, Reagan might have made an appeal for a comprehensive, impregnable shield part of his campaign for the presidency in 1980, but his advisers talked him out of it. It would be too controversial, they said; it would expose him to the charge that he was reckless and would plunge the United States into a fearsome new arms race if not a nuclear war.* Edward Teller, the "father" of the American hydrogen bomb and a friend of Reagan's, believed that the United States could develop the ultimate anti-weapon based in space. Lieutenant General Daniel O. Graham, the retired director of the Defense Intelligence Agency, was the moving force behind an organization called High Frontier, which promoted space-based defenses. He lobbied the President to "implement a basic change in U.S. grand strategy and make a 'technological end-run' on the Soviets." The Chief of Naval Operations, Admiral James Watkins, argued that a "moral imperative" compelled the United States to persist in the search for something better than mutual assured destruction (MAD). Reagan said that he, too, had been thinking a lot about the "immorality" of MAD. Isn't it better, he frequently asked, to save lives rather than to avenge them? The passage at the end of the March 23, 1983, speech was his way of saying to the American people: I don't like these awful weapons any more than you

*The 1980 Republican party platform—which had also called for the re-establishment of military and technological superiority over the Soviet Union—contained an appeal for a "vigorous research and development of an effective anti-ballistic missile system."

Four years later, when Reagan was running for re-election with the espousal of SDI behind him and very much part of his record, his Democratic opponent, Walter Mondale, was having little success in scoring points against Reagan with the traditional liberal complaint that SDI was destabilizing. So at one point Mondale was reduced to attacking the idea *from the right*—on the grounds that the President's offer someday to share SDI with the Soviet Union would mean giving American military secrets to the enemy.

do; support me on the MX in the near term, and in the long term, we'll come up with something better.

In addition, the deputy national security adviser at the time, Robert McFarlane, believed that the United States had an opportunity to exert leverage on the Soviets in arms control by threatening them with the prospect of a new arms race in an arena where the United States had economic and technological advantages.

The issue of strategic defense would almost certainly not have taken anything like the form it did had anyone else been President. Historians debate the relative influence on events of the great impersonal forces of history and of history's great and forceful personalities. In this case, the person made the difference. At the time that he introduced SDI to the world, Reagan had not given much thought to the historical or strategic arguments against doing so, in part because he was not well versed in those arguments to begin with. But, insofar as he was aware of them, they did not seem germane to what he was trying to accomplish. SDI was not the result of deep presidential immersion in the field of nuclear strategy; rather, it was a by-product of Reagan's political instincts at work. Those instincts told him that it was a good time to break out of what he found to be the rarefied, hidebound and profoundly gloomy thinking that had long dominated U.S. defense policy and diplomacy alike.

During his attempt to grapple with the unfamiliar and rather disagreeable subject of arms control in his first term, Reagan had displayed a characteristic that unnerved some of his advisers. He seemed uninterested in international relations as such. He showed little knowledge of, or even curiosity about, the interaction of states and forces in the world arena, and even less about the technical aspects of nuclear matters. It was as though the esoterica of weaponry and the big-think of strategy were things other people were paid to worry about. When counselors spoke to him about what the government ought to be doing, the goals it should set, and the methods it should employ, Reagan often seemed to tune out. The way to get his attention was to suggest what he personally should say about a foreign problem or policy. Then he would sit up and his eyes would come back into focus. What he cared about was speeches—particularly his own. He knew that his smooth delivery, his easygoing, winning manner and his ability to convey absolute conviction were big assets. He worked at fine-tuning his speeches with an enthusiasm that he rarely devoted to other duties.

He tended to see the announcement of a proposal or a policy as an end in itself. If the speech worked as a speech, then the policy for which it was a vehicle was a good one. If the speech came off, the policy could be sustained, whether it was an address to Evangelical Christians on the evil empire, the proclamation of a crusade for democracy delivered to the British Parliament, or an initiative that would, in a single stroke, repudiate the assumptions underlying the nuclear peace and, if it worked, render all Soviet missiles impotent and obsolete.

More than any other program in the area of foreign policy and national security, SDI bore Reagan's personal imprimatur. It was truly *his* initiative. Reagan believed that if a leader dares to ask elementary questions, the most intractable problems become amenable to solution; the leader's constituents suddenly feel that there is hope, that he embodies that hope, and that they are fortunate that he is in charge. Bold, simple schemes worked well for him as political rhetoric. He preferred to say, in effect: here's the problem—poverty, inflation, international terrorism, nuclear war; now here, in a simple declarative sentence, is the solution: let's do it. If the United States is running a dangerously large budget deficit, why not simply outlaw it by adopting an amendment to the Constitution requiring a balanced budget? If the nation is threatened by Soviet ballistic missiles, why not simply develop a system to shoot them down before they can do any harm?

This approach appealed to Reagan's image of Uncle Sam as an enterprising, self-sufficient, fix-it man with more trust in his own common sense than in what the know-it-alls might say. He always enjoyed a story about an eccentric inventor who tinkers for years in his garage with a gadget the neighbors chuckle over—until it whirrs and takes flight or otherwise changes the course of history.

SDI had yet another, more mundane political appeal for Reagan. It gave him a better position in the growing debate over the future both of arms control and of what was already termed the Reagan defense buildup. By early 1983 there were two developments that troubled the Administration. The arms-control negotiations in Geneva were in stalemate, with the possibility of a breakdown later in the year; and, partly because of that stalemate, the President's strategic modernization program faced increasing criticism on Capitol Hill. The nuclear freeze movement was, once again, beginning to gather force throughout the country. A year earlier, this same combination—growing congressional resistance to the MX and public interest in the freeze—had prompted Reagan to unveil his START proposal.

Now the President had an opportunity to say to the arms-controllers and pro-freeze forces, here is something better than what you have been asking for; you want to freeze or reduce levels of nuclear weapons; I want to abolish the threat altogether. It was a chance to co-opt the nuclear abolitionists.

Better still, SDI gave Reagan a way of holding out this promise without reopening the dismal prospect of yet another interminable and ultimately frustrating negotiation with the Soviets in Geneva. Arms-control proposals can have no impact except as exercises in public relations as long as the Soviets say *nyet*, which is one of their favorite words. By contrast, SDI was something the United States could do on its own. It was originally and essentially a unilateralist concept, and in that sense very much akin to the Reagan Doctrine.

THE MANY FACES OF SDI

In ancient Greek drama, when the plot could not be resolved satisfactorily, an actor playing a god would sometimes be lowered by a pulley onto the stage. He would bring supernatural powers to bear on the untidy affairs of mortals, imposing on the story a neat, if not necessarily happy, ending. Later, Roman literary critics called this device *deus ex machina*—the god from the machine. SDI served a similar purpose. It was a way of rewriting the story of the nuclear age so that it could have the ending that the President wanted. With a sweep of the wand of technology, the United States could free itself from the tangles of deterrence, vulnerability and arms control.

The films of Alfred Hitchcock frequently made use of another device, which Hitchcock called "the MacGuffin." The MacGuffin is the hollow center of the plot, the all-important something that everyone is looking for but that does not bear further explanation. It matters little how the thing will work, or indeed whether it will work; what matters is that it is mysterious, perhaps miraculous, and that everybody wants to find it and exploit it, whether for wealth or power or love. The MacGuffin might be a giant diamond, a Maltese falcon, a magic ring, or a holy grail. In *Torn Curtain* it is the secret formula for an anti-missile defense that the East German scientist alone knows and that Paul Newman, as the American spy, wants to find out.*

The *deus ex machina* of SDI eventually became a MacGuffin. The idea of strategic defense had many attractions for the President. But just what was it? What was to be defended? By what means? With how

---

*As recounted by David Freeman in *The Last Days of Alfred Hitchcock* (New York: Overlook Press, 1984, p. 51), the name MacGuffin comes from a story Hitchcock liked to tell about two men on a train. One says, "What's that up on the baggage rack?"

"Oh," the second man answers. "That's my MacGuffin."

"Well, what's a MacGuffin?"

"It's an apparatus for trapping lions in the Scottish Highlands," the second one says.

"But there aren't any lions in the Scottish Highlands," the first one answers.

"Well, then, that's no MacGuffin."

much reliability? What was the schedule for putting whatever machinery was necessary into place? What was the ultimate goal? Could it be realized? What was the operational relationship between strategic defense and strategic offense? How did it fit into arms control? In the absence of coherent and unified answers by the Administration to these questions, various constituencies affected by or involved in SDI used it to further their own aims much as Hitchcock used the secret formula to advance the plot of *Torn Curtain*.

President Reagan could set forth his vision; others would have to fulfill it. The March 1983 speech touched off a vigorous debate in the scientific, engineering, and strategic communities. While unresolved, that debate yielded a large body of forcefully articulated skepticism about whether the President's objective was feasible in the foreseeable future at any price, let alone one that American taxpayers would be willing to pay.

Judgments about about the feasibility of SDI depend on one's ability to imagine, first, a full-scale Soviet missile attack against the United States, then a multi-layered American defensive system that would thwart the attack, then the countermeasures that the Soviets might use to neutralize the American defenses, and finally the counter-countermeasures that the United States would use to protect its defenses.

The trajectory of an ICBM and its warheads proceeds in three stages. The "boost" phase lasts from the launch of the rocket to its exit from the atmosphere. In the mid-course phase, it travels outside the atmosphere from one continent to another, dispensing its warheads. The third and final stage is the re-entry, or terminal phase, when the warheads, each independently targeted, crash down on silos, airbases, or cities.

For the purposes of a comprehensive defense, the boost phase is crucial because the rockets have not yet released their multiple warheads. A single death-ray that destroys a single ICBM could prevent as many as ten enemy warheads from ever reaching their targets. Boost-phase interception has been compared to tackling the quarterback before he can throw the ball. Lasers were prominent candidates for this task, but some scientists favored concentrated beams of subatomic particles instead. Whatever the technology, it was bound to be expensive. Many installations—certainly dozens, perhaps hundreds—would be required to destroy the entire Soviet missile force. Even the strongest partisans of strategic defense admitted that some way would have to be found to produce the relevant technologies far more cheaply than was currently possible.

Defenses designed to destroy missiles in their boost phase could not be based in the relative safety of the defender's territory. If they did, by the time they were activated the attacker's weapons would already have reached the mid-course or perhaps even the reentry phase; the quarterback would have completed his pass, and his receiver would be heading into the end zone. The most logical deployment for boost-phase defenses would be for them to hover in space, above the territory of the U.S.S.R. If they were, they would themselves be exposed to harassment and possible destruction by the Soviets. Instead of beginning its first strike with a launch of its ICBMs against targets in the United States, the Soviet Union could begin by attacking SDI battlestations, clearing the way for the barrage of missile warheads. Laser-equipped platforms might defend American cities, but what would defend the defenders?

Moreover, the system would have to rely on as-yet unbuilt computers of unparalleled power and complexity to coordinate the main tasks of detecting the beginning of a Soviet attack, discriminating between real warheads and fake ones ("decoys"), training lasers on myriad, fast-moving targets, and verifying "kills"—all in a matter of seconds if not micro-seconds. The level of performance would have to be higher than that of any untested system of lesser complexity, and SDI could never be fully tested before it would have to work. If it did not work perfectly—if it only destroyed, for instance, 90 percent of the nuclear weapons that the Soviet Union fired at the United States in an attack using only 10 percent of its arsenal—the largest cities in North America could still lie in charred ruins half an hour after launch, with tens of millions of Americans dead or dying.

There was, in the opinion of some scientists, no useful precedent for what Reagan had proposed. Supporters recalled that John Kennedy had vowed to put a man on the moon, and despite a chorus of naysayers, the challenge had been met. Opponents of SDI replied that the moon had never shot back at the Apollo spacecraft. The Soviet Union was not going to sit and watch while the United States worked on SDI; it would do everything in its power to thwart the program.

Albert Einstein was once asked why man had been able to plumb the secrets of the universe and use what he discovered to make bombs of untold power but had not then had the wit to contrive political arrangements to make certain that the weapons would never be used. The reason, the great scientist replied, is that politics is more difficult than physics. In the case of strategic defense, the reverse seemed to be true: the politics was the easy part. The President made a speech; he proposed an idea that was simple to comprehend and appealing to contemplate; it received a generally favorable response. It was the physics that was difficult, and the engineering even more so.

For the President—but probably for him alone— the purpose of SDI was exactly as he had described it in March 1983: to render nuclear weapons impotent and obsolete; to accomplish general and complete nuclear disarmament; and to do so by the sheer force of America's know-how and can-do spirit.

A few years after his original speech, Reagan's idea had developed in a paradoxical way. On the one hand it had taken bureaucratic root in the American government. SDI had become an institution, with a budget, a director, an office, a constituency, and the continuing sponsorship of the President. On the other hand, the more they pondered the problem, the more skeptical many experts were that the United States could ever have the leakproof Astrodome of the President's vision. Not even the sunniest optimist in the SDI Organization (SDIO) of the Pentagon was prepared to say when, if ever, such a system would be available.

Many who were committed to the program nonetheless conceded, mainly in private, that a perfect, impregnable, comprehensive defense was not a realistic goal. Sometimes this concession came out in public. In a written response to a question put to him by the House Appropriations Committee, Lieutenant

General James Abrahamson, the director of SDIO, said, "Nowhere have we stated that the goal of the SDI is to come up with a 'leakproof' defense." George Keyworth, the President's science adviser and an early enthusiast for SDI, remarked in a *Washington Post* interview on December 24, 1984, "The SDI has never promised. . .absolute perfection, and the President would never propose such a bold step if only perfection would suffice."

Administration officials who left the government could be even more blunt. Richard DeLauer, the former Under Secretary of Defense for Research and Engineering, was downright caustic: "They were going to make nuclear weapons obsolete. But those of us who knew what was really going on couldn't support that. . .[The President's speech] was an overstatement with regard to how it would protect cities and the assertion that the protection would be leakproof."*

The President appeared not to be listening. A perfect defense was what he wanted, what he believed in, and what he thought he was getting. It was the personal vision of an immensely popular and therefore extremely powerful President. Uncritical support for SDI became the reigning orthodoxy within his Administration. As part of their political loyalty test, prospective appointees to high-level jobs, particularly at the Defense Department, were asked outright by the White House personnel office if they supported the President's program. An elaborate set of protocols evolved to govern the way in which Administration officials discussed the program. The Presi-

---

*DeLauer interviews in *The Los Angeles Times*, September 22, 1985, and *The Philadelphia Inquirer*, November 17, 1985.

dent, it was said, had posed a question. It was a legitimate question. Now the American scientific, industrial and military communities would join together to address that question and, in time, produce an answer. It would be intellectually shortsighted, arrogant, and irresponsible to prejudge the answer. Usually left unsaid, but always borne in mind, was the fact that the President himself had already prejudged the issue. In his March 1983 speech he had not only posed the challenge, he had declared his faith that the challenge could be met.

Even those who did not owe their jobs to Reagan were reluctant to take direct issue with him on the question of strategic defense. The belief was widespread, where SDI was concerned, that the emperor had no clothes; but no one would dare to say so. The various groups affected by the plan, therefore, found ways to argue that the outfit he was wearing suited their rather different tastes. They interpreted SDI in ways consistent with their own agendas, which were not at all consistent with one another.

The West Europeans were at first appalled at the President's idea. They were concerned that perfect defense was impossible but that the effort to achieve it would step up the arms race, creating strategic instability and even more intense East-West tension. The British Prime Minister, Margaret Thatcher, met with Reagan in December 1984, and together the two leaders issued a joint statement emphasizing that SDI did not represent a renunciation of deterrence or of existing agreements; it was a research program compatible with the SALT I ABM treaty of 1972, the only major arms-control treaty still formally in force between the superpowers, and that there would be no deployment without consultation with the allies and negotiation with the Soviets.

The Europeans also expressed their concern that if SDI did achieve its goal, it would have an isolationist effect, returning the United States to a pre-1941 mentality of Fortress America. The result would be the divorce, or "de-coupling," of their security from that of the United States. The Americans would be safe beneath their warhead-resistant shield, while the European allies would be all the more vulnerable to Soviet nuclear and conventional forces nearby. In response to this concern, the President revised his program to be "global" in scope: the space-based, boost-phase interceptors would have the capability of destroying SS-20s launched toward West Germany or Japan just as easily as SS-18s launched toward the United States.

Thus reassured that no sudden changes in the nuclear order were imminent, the Europeans could ignore the long-term strategic implications of the President's program and concentrate on the short-term economic opportunities that it presented. Their attitude toward SDI was like that of the man in the medieval court who, when condemned to death, promised that if the king spared his life, he would teach the monarch's favorite horse to talk within a year. The king agreed. A friend was shocked and said to the man, "What have you done? You know that you can't teach that horse to talk." The man replied, "You're right, I can't teach the horse to talk. But in a year anything can happen. I may die. The king may die. The horse may die. Or, who knows, the horse may learn to talk."

The European leaders knew that Reagan would not be in office after January 1989, well before a decision on deployment would be at hand. They could afford to regard SDI not as a potentially dangerous strategic innovation but as a large international pork-barrel project. The Defense Department invited the Europeans and the Japanese to participate. Most accepted.*

The President's political opponents at home were also skeptical, but the popular appeal of strategic defense was such that they did not launch a frontal attack on SDI. Instead, Congressional Democrats concentrated their efforts on questioning the budget for the program and insisting, much as Prime Minister Thatcher had done, that the research and development be conducted in compliance with existing arms-control agreements.

SDI had few true believers even within the ranks of the Administration. In fact, it divided the Administration, and along familiar lines. A division over arms control had existed since the President's first year in office. One faction, with its headquarters in the Office of the Secretary of Defense, was hostile to the entire undertaking. Its members argued forcefully in private, and occasionally intimated in public, that the enterprise was, by its very nature, dangerous for the United States. This was not, however, an argument that could be made palatable to the American Congress or public. So instead, people of this camp accused their predecessors of pursuing agreements for their own sake. The new Administration, they main-

---

*Except for the French, who proposed a European alternative to SDI to be called "Eureka."

tained, was not against arms control; rather, it was determined to hold arms control to a higher standard than in the past. They were not against dealing with the Soviets, they were for dealing with greater toughness—and for achieving better deals.

The most determined, skillful and articulate representative of this point of view was Richard Perle, the Assistant Secretary of Defense for International Security Policy.* The group Perle epitomized saw in SDI an opportunity to jettison both the process and product of arms control. SDI, they saw, was bound to come into conflict with the ABM treaty. Their aim was to provoke the clash sooner rather than later. They mounted their campaign on two fronts: one concerned space-based anti-missile defenses of a sort that would not be ready for deployment for many years or even decades; the other involved more modest land-based anti-missile defenses, which could be developed and deployed in the near term.

They contended, in effect, that because SDI envisioned technologies other than those that had been available when the ABM treaty was signed, the program was exempt from the treaty's constraints on development and testing of new ABM devices. At issue was the way in which the treaty dealt with ABMs "based on other physical principles"—a term meant to anticipate weapons utilizing directed energy or particle beams as opposed to interceptors that were fired from the ground and exploded near enough to an incoming warhead to destroy it. According to the traditional interpretation of the ABM treaty, the de-

*This characterization of Perle and the school of thought he represented is based on *Deadly Gambits*.

velopment and testing of exotic mobile or space-based systems were banned.*

But in 1985, Perle and others in the Administration who comprised the anti-arms-control faction claimed that the text of the treaty and the negotiating record were ambiguous on the question of whether the Soviet negotiators in SALT I had ever formally agreed on this point. They argued that this ambiguity left the treaty open to what came to be called the "permissive interpretation," as opposed to the restrictive one that had held sway for thirteen years. The Soviets, of course, would have little motivation to continue their compliance with a treaty that failed to constrain an all-out American program to develop large-scale strategic defenses based on high technology. That was just the point: the permissive interpretation would have the effect of sabotaging SALT because it would give the Soviets an incentive to break out of the ABM treaty (something that this faction contended they were doing anyway, with the Siberian radar and other alleged violations).

The second part of Perle's effort seemed intended to have much the same effect, but in a quite different way. He and like-minded officials reinterpreted SDI in a way that put it at odds with the ABM treaty in the near term. They explained that whatever grandiose vision the President might have for an Astrodome that would protect the entire Free World sometime in the twenty-first century, what SDI really meant, here and now, was something much more modest: the defense of American military targets, primarily

*The American military had made sure that the wording of the ABM treaty left open the possibility of developing and testing exotic technologies for fixed ground-based ABMs.

ICBM silos. Whatever dazzling experiments the Pentagon might want to carry out to prove that it could bounce lasers off mirrors in space, the protection of U.S. missile sites could be accomplished by less exotic, indeed perhaps even existing technologies, such as ground-based interceptors. Technologically, these would be latter-day versions of the ABMs of the 1960s. The rationale for deploying them was no different from the one underlying the deployment of their predecessors.

As early as February and March 1982, a full year before the President's SDI speech, Perle said in congressional testimony, "I would hope that were we to conclude that the only way we could defend our own strategic forces was by deploying defense, we would not hesitate to renegotiate the [1972 ABM] treaty and, failing Soviet acquiescence in that renegotiation, I would hope that we would abrogate the treaty." He called "the preclusion of strategic defense" by the ABM treaty "destabilizing" and a "mistake."

Perle's comments were echoed and amplified in many other Administration suggestions that the near-term goal of SDI was traditional defense of ICBM silos rather than exotic and much more comprehensive defenses of the civilian population. A White House publication on SDI released in January 1985 said that "providing a better, more stable basis for enhanced deterrence is the central purpose of the SDI program." A Pentagon report to Congress around the same time said, "With defenses, the U.S. seeks not to replace deterrence, but to enhance it." In an address to the National Press Club on May 1, 1984, Secretary of Defense Weinberger said, "The ultimate goal of the Strategic Defense Initiative is to develop thoroughly reliable defenses." But in his next sentence, he added, "This does not preclude, of course, any intermediate deployment that could provide, among other things, defense of the offensive deterrent forces, which of course we still have to maintain."

George Keyworth, the President's science adviser who had been such a vigorous proponent of SDI in its most grandiose form, stated on a television program in August 1984, "We are not saying that we can suddenly defuse a nuclear weapon, or the threat. What we are talking about is restoring stability and making nuclear war far less likely." In an article later that year, Keyworth asked, "Do we want to abandon deterrence? Even though many critics may state that those of us who advocate strategic defense are calling for such a policy, there is no question that we must retain a specific retaliatory capability."

Fred Iklé, the Under Secretary of Defense for Policy, who was a close ally of Perle's, remarked in testimony on Capitol Hill in February 1985, "The initial phases of a missile defense, on the road to a more complete deployment, would enhance stability, the stability of our present deterrent forces." Shortly afterward, Iklé added, "The Department of Defense has, of course, been examining for some time how strategic defensive systems could, depending on future research results, be integrated into our overall deterrent posture."*

*Keyworth, CBS program "Crossroads," August 15, 1984, and "The Case for Strategic Defense: An Option for a World Disarmed," *Issues in Science and Technology*, Fall, 1984; Iklé, New York Times, June 1, 1985, and testimony before Senate Armed Services Committee, February 21, 1985.

Perhaps so-called "terminal defenses"—principally ground-based interceptors that attacked incoming enemy warheads in their terminal phase, before they could reach their targets—could be augmented later by space-based devices for destroying enemy missiles in their boost phase. But the challenges to technology and budget alike were considerably less onerous if the goal was to defend silos rather than cities. The deployment of such a system could come in the relatively near future; it would also be an obvious violation of the ABM treaty. Once again, that seemed to be just the point. While there was no admission of these goals on the record, the objectives and requirements of SDI were being redefined in a way that put the program on a collision course with arms control.

This revisionism was inconsistent with the President's view on SDI. If SDI served to enhance the survivability of the United States' deterrent forces, it was difficult to see how it could simultaneously advance the cause of eliminating the need for those forces. If defense was a means of making sure that offensive missiles could survive a preemptive attack, it was also a way of assuring that they would never become impotent and obsolete.

Some other members of the Administration were more favorably disposed to arms control. Toward the end of 1983, and the end of START, there was an attempt from this quarter to make the American position more negotiable by offering tradeoffs between systems in which the United States had an edge (bombers and cruise missiles) and those in which Soviet reductions were desirable (ICBMs). But this faction was too weak and too much on the defensive within the bureaucracy to prevail. Its attempts at moderating the American position in START failed, and the Soviets withdrew from negotiations at the end of 1983.

People of this predisposition saw SDI as a means of getting that better deal. In the rosiest of scenarios, SDI might even become the key to the best deal ever in arms control, which was sometimes called the grand compromise. The Soviets would undertake significant reductions in their most threatening weapons in exchange for constraints on an American program that was still only a gleam in the President's eye.

The view that SDI could help the United States achieve significant and stabilizing reductions in strategic offensive forces was best represented by Paul Nitze. In some ways Nitze was a paragon of what the Administration considered virtues; in others, he was an apostate, a renegade, and for that reason a hero to the Administration's critics. In his long career, Nitze had frequently staked out the hard-line position in the debate of the day over the Soviet threat and what to do about it. In 1950 he had been the principal author of National Security Council Memorandum Number 68, one of the key documents of the Cold War, and in 1957 of the Gaither Report, which raised concerns about the danger of a Soviet first strike. In the 1970s he was a member of Team B, a panel of conservative outsiders that accused the Central Intelligence Agency of underestimating the Soviet threat. He was a founding member of the Committee on the Present Danger, a private group that lobbied for an American military buildup, and a forceful critic of the SALT II treaty. More than any other single American, he had been responsible for generating concern about the "window of vulnerability" and doubts about the efficacy of traditional arms control. Largely for that reason he was invited to join the Reagan Administration, originally as the chief negotiator in the Intermediate-range Nuclear Forces (INF) talks of 1981–83.

But he was never fully accepted, or trusted, by the Administration's hard-core opponents of arms control, such as Perle. As one of the principal negotiators of the SALT I ABM treaty, Nitze had been an arms-controller himself, and they feared that he would show his true colors once again. This he did during the INF talks. In one of the most controversial and intriguing episodes of the first Reagan Administration, Nitze embarked in 1982 on an unauthorized exploratory negotiation with his Soviet counterpart in Geneva—the so-called "walk in the woods"—and arrived at a compromise that many believed would have been advantageous to the West had it been accepted.* As it happened, it was rejected, both in Washington (where Perle led the opposition) and in Moscow. That incident helped make Nitze the champion of the pro-arms-control faction within the Administration and the *bête noire* of the opponents.

In the second Reagan Administration, Nitze, who enjoyed the confidence of George Shultz, served as special adviser to the President and Secretary of State. While Perle was attempting to use SDI to block arms control, Nitze was trying just as hard to use SDI to advance arms control. His premise seemed to be that the Soviets leaders might be so concerned about an American program to develop and deploy large-scale strategic defenses based on high technology that

*See *Deadly Gambits*, pp. 116–51.

they would propose, in exchange for restrictions on that program, significant reductions in their offensive weaponry. Then perhaps the President would be sufficiently attracted to those reductions that he would agree to constraints on SDI.

Nitze endorsed the President's dream of a nuclear-weapons-free world. That put his position in marked contrast to Perle's, allowing him to dismiss the idea of the unilateral American defense of silos as the near-term goal of SDI and resist pressure to break out of the ABM treaty in the near future.

In 1985, Nitze formulated the so-called "strategic concept," a brief statement that set forth a timetable for arms reductions. The ultimate goal was to be the one cherished by the President, "the elimination of nuclear arms." Before that, there would be a period of "transition," in which the levels of offensive weaponry on both sides would be reduced while levels of defense would be increased. More immediately, in the next ten years, the objective of American policy would be "a radical reduction in the power of existing and planned offensive nuclear arms, as well as the stabilization of the relationship between offensive and defensive nuclear arms, whether on earth or in space." While arms control was not mentioned explicitly, the stated goals of reduction, stabilization and transition all strongly implied accommodation with the U.S.S.R. Thus the strategic concept was an alternative both to the unilateralist essence of SDI in its original form and to SDI as a way of defending missiles in their silos, as favored by Perle. The strategic concept was enshrined in a formal presidential directive, but it continued to be the subject of debate within the Administration.

The same happened with three criteria that Nitze said SDI would have to meet if it were ever to be deployed: it would have to be successful in thwarting a massive enemy attack; it would have to be survivable (there could be no means of preemptively blinding, disabling or destroying it); and it would have to be "cost-effective at the margins" (it would have to be cheaper to enhance the defenses than to mount offensive countermeasures).

That was a tall order. Nitze seemed to be defining the task of SDI in such a way as to assure that it would remain a research program and would not proceed to advanced development, testing and deployment. Perle saw Nitze's moves as just such a tactic and struck back. In an outbreak of semantic warfare between the two factions in 1986, the Pentagon tried at one point to replace the criterion of cost-effectiveness with that of "affordability," a more subjective term and therefore a less demanding requirement.

Thus, while Perle wanted to use SDI to force a breakout from the nuclear status quo, Nitze and Shultz, with the support of McFarlane, were treating SDI as a means of applying pressure on the Soviets to roll back their offensive buildup, thereby revalidating and reinforcing that status quo. If SDI accomplished this, it would be, as one presidential adviser put it, "the greatest sting operation in history": the abstract possibility of an American space-based defense would so terrify the Soviets that, in order to stave off the danger, they would finally show some restraint and accept reductions in their offensive capability.

The Shultz-Nitze camp persuaded the President to incorporate as part of his standard exposition on SDI a reiteration of the disclaimer he had made earlier at

Margaret Thatcher's behest: that SDI was a research program being conducted in compliance with the ABM treaty as narrowly, or restrictively, interpreted. That formulation allowed the United States to preserve the existing arms-control regime while still playing upon the Soviets' anxieties about the consequences for the long-term survivability and cost-effectiveness of their offensive forces if there were ever a breakthrough in American defensive technology. It also kept open the possibility that if the Soviets sufficiently reduced their offensive weapons, Reagan might eventually be able to accommodate their demands on defense simply by reiterating, yet again, that SDI was a research program conducted in compliance with the ABM treaty—only this time in a document co-signed by Gorbachev.

THE KREMLIN PROPOSES

The Soviet leaders grew alarmed and indignant as the idea of strategic defense gathered momentum in the United States. In response, Moscow began a public campaign, like the one that had failed to block the intermediate-range missiles from being based in Germany and Great Britain, to encourage political opposition to Star Wars in the West. Soviet spokesmen warned of the dangers of spreading the arms race into space. They accused the United States of seeking military superiority. There was no question in their minds as to whose nuclear weapons Reagan wanted to render impotent and obsolete. A leak-proof system of defense would indeed give the United States a commanding position in the superpower rivalry. The great achievement of the Brezhnev generation would be nullified. The keystone in the arch of Moscow's world position would be abruptly removed. The men in the Kremlin would no longer preside over one of the world's two superpowers. They would instead have on their hands a sprawling, backward, multinational empire with millions of mutinous subjects. And they would face a coalition of countries far more powerful than they in industrial productivity, which would once again be—as it had been before the advent of nuclear weapons—the basis of military strength.

This was, from the Soviet perspective, the worst case. How seriously the Kremlin leadership took the prospect of an effective space shield over North America is not easy to say. Soviet scientists and publicists produced their own version of American reports arguing that defense was not technically feasible. But the Soviets have always been great believers in American technological prowess. Sometimes they have seemed to have more faith in Yankee ingenuity than Americans themselves.

Even short of the worst case, moreover, SDI was an unattractive, even ominous prospect for the Kremlin. If the United States deployed a space shield, the Soviet Union would have to respond. If the Soviets were unwilling to stop supporting distant client states with little strategic or political value, they were hardly likely to ignore a military development that threatened their homeland itself. They would have to be able to defeat whatever defenses the United States put into space and might even attempt to match them.

To be sure, the Soviets were by no means total innocents with regard to strategic defense, their own propaganda to the contrary notwithstanding. They had the world's only deployed ABM system defending their capital (the one system allowed by the ABM treaty, for the American system had long since been taken out of service). The Soviet anti-aircraft network was far larger than its American counterpart and on hair-trigger alert (as the world was so gruesomely reminded by the shoot-down of the Korean airliner). Moreover, the Soviets were engaged in vigorous research, development and testing of ABM devices and possible components of a larger network. The Krasnoyarsk radar was only the most flagrant example of activities that called into question their compliance with the SALT I treaty.

Still, there was no reason to believe that they were ready, much less eager, to embark in an all-out SDI race with the United States. A head-to-head competition in strategic defense would force the Soviet-American rivalry into the realm of high technology, where the Soviets trailed far behind the West. In the non-nuclear confrontation in Europe, the Soviets could make up in numbers what they lacked in quality. NATO's tanks and planes might be more sophisticated, its soldiers more committed to the cause for which they would have to fight. But the Warsaw Pact could field more of each. Soviet scientists and engineers were not as creative or as skillful at designing and producing nuclear weapons as their American counterparts. But they did not have to be, for the American advantages would not prevent the destruction of the continental United States in a nuclear exchange. Nuclear weapons were blunt instruments, a Soviet specialty. However, if it came to building complicated systems of radars, space platforms, computers and lasers, the peculiar disabilities of the Stalinist economic system would count for a great deal.

Even if they did not try to match American developments in strategic defense, and even if they concluded that American defenses were going to be only partially effective, the Soviets would still have to overhaul much of their existing offensive arsenal. The exteriors of ICBMs would have to be thickened and the boost phase accelerated in order to make them less vulnerable to lasers; warheads would have to be proliferated, made maneuverable, and masked with decoys and other so-called penetration aids in order to be sure of getting through terminal-phase American defenses. All this would be expensive, perhaps ruinously so.

Soviet resources were already stretched. Even without a new round of the arms race, the leaders were, because of their many domestic difficulties, under pressure. A space race would make a bad situation much worse.

Still, the debate over SDI forced the Soviets, in a way that they had never been forced before and that certainly did not come easily to them, to examine why that status quo was in jeopardy. It drove home to them that while they had been accumulating weapons for the past twenty years, the Americans had been accumulating anxieties. In the United States, as the Soviets knew only too well, anxiety is often the mother of invention; and American inventions are invariably bad news for the Soviet Union.

By 1984 Gorbachev and his comrades seemed willing to go the next step and ask themselves what they might have to do in order to avert a world in which high tech ran free on the high frontier. They proposed arms-control measures that were more conciliatory than any the Soviet Union had made, or even considered, in the past. Soviet anxieties too, it seemed, could be the mother of invention. Goaded by SDI, the Soviets themselves became, for the first time, initiators in arms control. Gorbachev seemed particularly adept at capitalizing on the opportunities for propaganda that went with his new office. In 1985–86, for example, the Kremlin took the lead in proposing to the Americans ways out of the stalemate in arms control. Their proposals were replete with tricks, traps and teasers, but they also contained some potentially important concessions.

When the Soviets began to look for ways to return to the talks from which they had withdrawn after their failure to block the American Euromissile deployments, they put SDI at the center of their proposals. Their fear of SDI had something to do with their return to the negotiating table they had left at the end of 1983, but there were other reasons as well. Walking out of the talks in Geneva had done nothing for the Soviet leaders in the eyes of international public opinion. As early as mid-1984, during the American presidential election, Moscow was angling for a way to get talks started again, and SDI figured prominently as the pretext for doing so. On June 29 of that year, they offered to begin negotiations with the goal of banning space weapons. The United States responded promptly that it would join such talks if there were a broader arms-control agenda. The U.S.S.R. denounced the American attempt to impose a "precondition" and rejected the broadened talks. Thus in this phase of the pre-negotiation maneuvers, the United States appeared willing to trade defense for offense, while the Soviets seemed unwilling.

The Soviet stance began to change about six months later. In January 1985, shortly before the second Reagan inaugural and during the last days of Konstantin Chernenko, Shultz and Andrei Gromyko, who was still Foreign Minister, met in Geneva. They agreed to new negotiations under a complicated formula whereby each side would send a single delegation to Geneva, but the negotiations would be held in three subgroups—one on INF, another on strategic weapons, and the third on defensive and space systems. As Shultz and Gromyko haggled over a communiqué, the Soviet side pressed hard for a statement that these three issues would be resolved "in their inter-relationship."

At the Geneva summit in November 1985, Gorbachev spent much of the time making the Soviet case against SDI. Reagan was amiable but unyielding. He tried to persuade the Soviet leader that defense would be good for both sides. By not giving an inch on SDI, Reagan earned the applause of his constituents on the right, who might otherwise have criticized him for going to the summit, exchanging handshakes and smiles, and signing a communiqué with the leader of the Soviet Union.

Gorbachev brought a new level of ingenuity and persistence to the Soviet conduct of arms control. He doubtless realized the economic as well as the military threat that SDI posed, and he knew how little the society over which he now presided could afford additional economic burdens. SDI was a long-term challenge, and, unlike his immediate predecessors, Gorbachev had every hope of being a long-term incumbent. Throughout 1985 and into 1986, his government hurled at Washington a dizzying barrage of proposals. Some were merely cynical headline-grabbers, some were suggestions for formal treaty language, and some were feelers advanced by *institutchiki* and other quasi- or crypto-officials. But the rough contours of what Moscow might be willing to offer to reach a compromise began to emerge in late 1985 and became clearer in 1986.

On June 11, 1986, the Soviets presented a new proposal at the negotiating table in Geneva. They discarded some of the more patently unacceptable aspects of their position (such as an insistence that U.S. intermediate-range nuclear forces be deemed strategic weapons since they were capable of reaching the Soviet Union from the territory of American allies or from American aircraft carriers). They also expressed a willingness to make unprecedented reductions in their offensive forces. The key feature in their emerging proposal was an offer to reduce significantly their ICBM warheads.

The Soviets were moving in the direction that Reagan had sought to induce them to go in START during his first term. His only leverage then had been the prospect of an American offensive buildup. The Soviets had been willing to risk an "offense-offense" arms race rather than bargain away some of their existing weapons for American promises not to build weapons still in the planning stage. But the prospect of an "offense-defense" race was apparently another matter.

Hence, there was a steady stream of increasingly forthcoming offers in Geneva, amplified and sweetened by less formal hints of even greater concessions still to come. At the same time, the Soviets scaled back their demand for restrictions on defense. When Shultz and Gromyko met in Geneva in January 1985, the Soviets wanted to ban not only development and testing but also research on "space-strike arms," a term they defined in a way that was so comprehensive and one-sided it might have meant the cancellation of the space shuttle. Then, in his interview in August 1985 with *Time* Magazine, Gorbachev said that what he called "fundamental" research would not be covered by the ban. But Soviet officials subsequently explained that "purposeful" research on strategic defenses would still be forbidden. Since purpose would be a matter of declared intention, the American SDI would be outlawed, while the Soviets could justify the continued testing of huge high-energy lasers in Central Asia by claiming that they were for medical purposes. In the spring of 1986 the Soviets began exploring ways to restrict SDI by reaffirming the ABM treaty.

By June 1986, Administration national-security policies in general and SDI in particular were in trouble on the home front. There was an uproar on Capitol Hill and among the West European allies over the presidential decision to break with SALT II at the end of the year. Many in Congress sought to hold funding for SDI hostage to the restoration of a promising arms-control process. It was increasingly apparent that Reagan would pay a political price if there were no return engagement with Gorbachev.

In a series of statements, Reagan markedly adjusted his approach. Having disparaged so many earlier Soviet offers, he had kind and hopeful words about the latest one, which had, indeed, represented significant movement on the part of the Kremlin. He backed off from the SALT II breakout, saying that the decision was tentative and that he might reconsider it in the light of Soviet behavior in the negotiations. He stressed that even if SALT II did pass into history, he had high hopes, and every intention, of replacing it with a new pact. In answer to questions, he dropped broad hints that SDI might, after all, be negotiable as part of an offense-defense tradeoff of the sort the Soviets were proposing in Geneva.

In a presidential letter to Gorbachev during the summer, and in accompanying statements that his aides and envoys were authorized to make to their Soviet counterparts, the Administration tried to signal that SDI was, in some sense, negotiable. In what sense it was negotiable was not clear even to Administration policymakers themselves, not to mention to the Soviets. The President was still committed to eventual deployment. But perhaps deployment could be delayed; perhaps there could be agreement on the level and nature of development and testing that would be permissible in the meantime. The Soviets were invited to interpret the ambiguous, almost cryptic position that the President took in his letter as a sign of flexibility, a hint of greater flexibility yet to come. The Soviets were more inclined to interpret the letter as further evidence of the division and ambivalence that still wracked the Administration.

They may have been right. Their skepticism was hardly allayed when, at the end of the summer, an American delegation headed by Nitze and including Perle arrived in Moscow to elaborate on the presidential letter. The differences between the two governments and within the American government might yet prevent a compromise of any kind in the realm of strategic offense and defense.

President Reagan seemed to want such a compromise if it could possibly be negotiated, but the terms he would accept were unclear. In a speech to a high school graduating class on June 19, he said that in their latest proposals, "the Soviets have begun to make a serious effort"; and he was hoping that, at a meeting later in the year, Gorbachev would "join me in taking action – action in the name of peace." He gave that speech in Glassboro, New Jersey, where nineteen years before, Lyndon Johnson and Robert McNamara began the SALT process by trying to persuade Aleksei Kosygin that strategic arms control depended on limiting defense and offense alike.

Despite the choice of Glassboro as the site of the speech, the President was not signaling his acceptance of Johnson and McNamara's basic message to Kosygin: that strategic defense was undesirable. Quite the contrary, Reagan made clear that he had not given up his enthusiasm for the promise of SDI, calling it a "shield that could protect us from nuclear missiles just as a roof protects a family from rain."

Thus the President's evolution was incomplete and ambiguous. In 1983, his political instincts had told him that SDI was an attractive alternative to arms control. Three years later, his instincts seemed to be telling him that SDI might be a useful part of arms control. But that did not mean that he was yet, or necessarily ever would be, willing to give up entirely the program and the dream it represented.

5

REYKJAVIK AND BEYOND

The late summer and autumn of 1986 were a busy, confusing and dramatic period in Soviet-American relations. Within four months, the tone and substance of communications between Washington and Moscow oscillated sharply between conciliation and acrimony. At issue was whether there would be a second meeting between Ronald Reagan and Mikhail Gorbachev. If summitry futures had been traded like commodities, fortunes would have been made and lost. The two leaders themselves engaged in a kind of arbitrage, trying to make quick political profits from the swings of the market.

In July and August the President and the General Secretary exchanged letters and dispatched delegations of arms-control experts to each other's capitals. Momentum seemed to be building toward a summit in Washington at the end of the year. Then an American journalist was arrested in Moscow. Suddenly the mood soured, and the momentum slowed. But in the midst of what turned out to be a minor crisis, Reagan and Gorbachev made clear first to each other and then to the world that they were determined to proceed with the business between them. They agreed to hold a meeting that turned out to be one of the most extraordinary encounters in the history of the relations between their countries, perhaps in the annals of diplomacy.

The two-day meeting in Reykjavik, Iceland, on October 11-12, 1986, broke with virtually all the precedents of U.S.-Soviet relations. There were scarcely any preparations. The meeting that took place was entirely different from the one the Americans had expected. They had anticipated not a full-fledged summit, but, in President Reagan's phrase, "the last base camp" on the way to a Washington summit. Yet the agenda turned out to be much broader and the issues discussed far more consequential than even those the Americans had envisioned for the anticipated summit itself.

In some obvious ways, the Reykjavik meeting was a failure. At least in the short term, it derailed the summit process and dramatized the fragility of the U.S.-Soviet relationship. Not since Nikita Khrushchev refused to meet with Dwight Eisenhower in Paris in 1960 and argued with John Kennedy in Vienna the following year had an encounter between the American and Soviet leader ended so badly. In Iceland, when Reagan emerged from his final session with Gorbachev, his usual jaunty manner was missing; his mood was grim.

In reporting to the American press immediately afterward, Secretary of State George Shultz appeared exhausted, dejected and defeated. He had to fight to control his emotions. He repeatedly used the word "disappointment" to describe the weekend. The

White House Chief of Staff, Donald Regan, at an impromptu press conference at Keflavik airport, lashed out at the Soviets, saying that "they finally showed their hand. It showed them up for what they are." He said that "there will not be another summit in the near future as far as I can see."

Despite the spectacular collapse of the meeting and the ensuing acrimony, there was also significant, if tentative, progress on arms control. In his press conference, Shultz spoke of "potential agreements" that were "breathtaking." The two sides had moved closer to accommodation on a range of issues than their top officials had considered possible beforehand.

In violation of all the conventional wisdom about sound negotiating tactics and prudent diplomacy, Reagan and Gorbachev engaged each other on the biggest, most difficult issue dividing them—how to structure and limit their huge stockpiles of nuclear weapons—and proceeded to improvise. Working groups of experts with no clear instructions toiled through the night to hammer out compromises on matters that years of negotiation had failed to resolve. The two leaders themselves spontaneously tabled variations on one of the oldest, most implausible and least productive themes of the nuclear age—general and complete disarmament. But they also spent considerable time adjusting their proposals for more practical measures that could become part of achievable, verifiable agreements.

They failed at the last minute to overcome the principal obstacle to a treaty that might have significantly reduced levels of offensive weaponry on both sides. They could not resolve the question of how, if at all, to constrain SDI. Gorbachev insisted that the program would give the United States military-technical superiority and a first-strike capability against the U.S.S.R. President Reagan insisted just as forcefully that SDI would produce a purely defensive shield against offensive nuclear forces and was therefore the moral alternative to traditional deterrence based on mutual assured destruction. Neither leader would accept the other's reasoning.

But the meeting did offer a glimmer of hope of a world in which the United States and its allies would be less threatened by Soviet ballistic missiles. It also demonstrated that SDI gives the United States considerable leverage in the effort to achieve such a world through arms control.

THE ROAD TO REYKJAVIK

The Reykjavik encounter was, in a sense, Gorbachev's revenge for the Geneva summit of a year earlier. The most important feature of that first meeting for Gorbachev was what had *not* happened: Reagan had come to the summit and gone home without yielding even the slightest concession on SDI, the American policy that most concerned the Soviet leaders. The General Secretary may have run into trouble when he arrived home in Moscow empty-handed. His comrades among the Kremlin old guard and the military could not have been pleased that the summit had failed to stop or even slow down SDI.

As a result of whatever displeasure he encountered in the Politburo, Gorbachev may have decided never again to let himself be lured to a summit at which SDI would be finessed. Throughout much of 1986 the two leaders engaged in a slow-motion fencing match over whether they would hold the second meeting to which they had agreed. The White House wanted the second meeting, which was to take place in the United States in June 1986 and in any case no later than September, before the November congressional elections.

The Kremlin made clear that it was not interested in another meeting without concrete progress in arms control. Soviet spokesmen said that June was much too soon for the necessary preparations and suggested that their leader would renege altogether on his promise to attend a second summit rather than participate in little more than another photo opportunity.

Even as they seemed to be stalling on a second summit, the Soviets stepped up their propaganda on behalf of a moratorium on all nuclear testing and a phased reduction of nuclear weapons that would lead to their elimination by the end of the century. These proposals were designed for maximum appeal to international public opinion. Each was also a way of attacking SDI. A comprehensive test ban would prevent the development of the nuclear-driven X-ray laser, which some scientists think is the most promising technology for space-based defenses; the elimination of offensive nuclear weapons within fifteen years would seem to make strategic defense all but superfluous. At the same time, however, the Soviets were also making their concrete concessions at the ongoing arms-control negotiations in Geneva.

By appearing to insist on progress in arms control as a condition for holding the summit, the Soviets were trying to exert political and psychological pressure on Reagan, whose interest in another meeting and in an arms-control accord was evident from his statements during the spring and summer. Time was running out for him. By 1987, even if his personal popularity remained high, the United States would be deep into the presidential campaign. It would be more difficult than usual to conduct foreign policy. Policy toward the Soviet Union would be especially vulnerable to the partisan and ideological passions of the election season. Moreover, growing public and congressional concerns over the federal budget deficit threatened a backlash against military spending, including spending on SDI.

If Reagan was to leave the presidency in a blaze of superpower statesmanship, he might need a second summit in late 1986 and another before leaving office. Moscow was attempting to get American arms-control concessions in exchange for keeping to the agreed schedule.

In September, Gorbachev complained in an interview with the Czechoslovak Communist Party newspaper *Rude Pravo*, "We have not moved an inch closer to an arms reductions agreement, despite all the efforts made by the U.S.S.R."

Even as they set conditions for another Reagan-Gorbachev meeting, however, the Soviets were evidently looking for a way to justify one. For a while they seemed to abandon, or at least loosen, the connection that they had made earlier among the various arms control negotiations. Although in January 1985 Gromyko had insisted that the three issues of intermediate-range nuclear forces (INF), strategic arms, and space and defensive systems had to be addressed simultaneously, starting with the Reagan-Gorbachev summit of November 1985, Soviet officials began saying that they would be willing to settle for an interim INF agreement, progress toward a nuclear test ban or perhaps even so-called confidence-building measures such as strengthened procedures for avoiding the accidental start of a war in Europe.

The Soviets seemed, in short, ambivalent about a summit. They did not want to allow the President's supporters to claim, as they had after the Geneva meeting, that standing tall and holding firm had paid off and that Gorbachev had knuckled under to Reagan. At the same time, they were worried about the consequences of yet another breakdown in Soviet-American diplomacy. Despite their professed fidelity to a great revolutionary tradition, the men in the Kremlin are extremely conservative. They are deeply uncomfortable with discontinuity, uncertainty, unpredictability. The failure to hold a follow-up summit would involve all three. And they were genuinely worried about the future of the nuclear competition. A respite from—or perhaps a long-term arrangement for the regulation of—that competition was necessary if Gorbachev was to have the *peredyshka*, or breathing space, that he seemed to need in order to carry out his domestic program.

The Soviets had to calculate the likely impact of the course of American politics on their interests. As the end of his presidency approached, Reagan would become a lame duck. Some Soviet officials said that their leaders were tempted simply to wait out what they called "this impossible Administration" and hope for someone more "reasonable." But given their penchant for worst-case analysis, Soviet officials had to consider at least the possibility that the next American President would be even more strident in criticizing their political system, more vigorous in attacking their empire on its flanks, perhaps even more committed to strategic defense. As they surveyed the American political landscape they could see a number of potential presidential candidates who seemed to fit that description. In discussions with Americans, Soviet specialists on the United States showed deep curiosity about the presidential prospects of Representative Jack Kemp and Senator Paul Laxalt.

Moreover, the difficulties that the Soviets had experienced with Reagan gave him a certain political advantage in managing the domestic politics of an agreement if one were achieved. He would have little trouble getting a treaty ratified by the Senate. Thus, both Reagan and Gorbachev had incentives to meet again.

The two leaders seemed to be moving in the direction of a second summit when they were jolted by one of the unforeseen events that have made the conduct of Soviet-American relations so accident-prone over the years. The episode started with a scene out of a Grade B film about the FBI, which was followed by one from an equally hackneyed thriller about the KGB. On August 23, Gennady Zakharov, a Soviet scientist on the staff of the United Nations, was arrested by the FBI while attempting to purchase intelligence secrets from an agent who had been working for the FBI. While he was the victim of this particular entrapment, Zakharov was clearly engaged in espionage. The KGB retaliated by setting a superficially similar trap in Moscow for Nicholas Daniloff, the correspondent for *U.S. News & World Report*. One of his Soviet contacts arranged for a meeting on August 30, at which he gave Daniloff a sealed envelope. Secret policemen then suddenly appeared, arrested Daniloff and claimed that the envelope contained state secrets. Unlike Zakharov, Daniloff did not know what he was receiving and had no thought of buying information. He was the victim of a primitive frame-up. The Soviets then tried to arrange a trade of Daniloff for their own man.

As some Soviets admitted privately, their government seriously underestimated the outrage that the Daniloff affair would provoke in the United States. The Reagan Administration's initial reaction was mild compared to that of the American media. This was not surprising, since one of their own was being held hostage. Congress, too, took a harder line than the White House, with some members insisting that all business with Moscow stop until Daniloff was set free.

In late September, Soviet Foreign Minister Eduard Shevardnadze came to the United States to take part in the opening session of the United Nations General Assembly and met with President Reagan and Secretary of State Shultz. Both sides had hoped the meetings would lay the groundwork for a summit. But Daniloff's imprisonment poisoned the atmosphere and complicated the agenda of the meetings. The potential effects of the whole affair seemed absurdly out of proportion to the cause.

Because of the depth of hostility and mistrust between the superpowers, Soviet-American relations often appear to exemplify Murphy's Law: whatever can go wrong, does go wrong—and at the worst possible time. Over the years, much has gone wrong, often scuttling the best-laid plans of statesmen on both sides. The U-2 incident of May 1960 led Khrushchev to storm out of the Paris summit; in response to the Soviet invasion of Czechoslovakia in August 1968, the United States postponed the opening of SALT; the invasion of Afghanistan virtually guaranteed that the U.S. Senate would not ratify the SALT II treaty; and the downing of the Korean airliner in September 1983 impeded George Shultz's effort to re-engage the U.S.S.R. in quiet diplomacy on a variety of bilateral and regional issues.

For all the differences among them, these incidents had three important features in common, which they shared with the Daniloff affair. First, the Kremlin's concern with security almost always takes precedence over propaganda and diplomacy. Moscow was determined to keep loyal Communists in power in Prague and Kabul no matter what the price in international opprobrium, just as it was determined to get its agent out of an American jail by any means necessary. Second, if what the Soviets do leads to a crisis in their relations with the United States, they are quick to blame Washington. And third, the disruption in relations has always proved temporary. On September 29, Daniloff was released as part of a compromise whereby Zakharov, too, was to be returned home, but not in a direct exchange.

The Daniloff affair was all too characteristic both of the Soviet Union itself and of the Soviet challenge to American policy. It illustrated anew the nature of the Soviet system: the institutionalization of paranoia and xenophobia that find expression in a deep animosity toward foreign journalists; the corruption of the law; the obsession with exposing enemies and, in the absence of real enemies, with finding and framing scapegoats instead. The Soviet system performs these tasks so well that it does other things badly. A state that defines internal security almost exclusively in terms of the power of the police finds it all too easy to give short shrift, not to mention inadequate resources, to other forms of security, such as economic well-being. The stock Soviet euphemism for the KGB is the "competent organs," the unintended implication being that all other organs are incompetent, which is not altogether wrong.

Thus, the Daniloff incident served to remind many Americans that the basis of their objections to the other superpower runs deeper than American opposition to the U.S.S.R.'s expansionism and its threatening military programs. Soviet foreign policy is objectionable largely because the Soviet Army and its rear guard of commissars, diplomats and propagandists have treated the people of Afghanistan, Poland, and Czechoslovakia in much the same way that the KGB treated Nicholas Daniloff—and, for that matter, Andrei Sakharov, Yuri Orlov (the dissident who was released from a labor camp and allowed to emigrate as part of the resolution of the Daniloff affair), and so many others.

During the episode, Reagan received considerable criticism from the right for proceeding with the Shultz-Shevardnadze meeting, for trying to keep plans for a summit on track, and generally for continuing "business as usual" with a regime that was holding captive an innocent American. But business as usual with the Soviet Union was, by definition, limited business, driven by the superpowers' mutual interest in the avoidance of war and by very little else. It was the kind of business that had historically proceeded, albeit with delays and distractions, even in the face of episodes far more serious than the Daniloff affair. If the United States refused to do business with the Soviet Union until Moscow began to treat decently its people, foreign journalists, and the citizens of neighboring countries, then no superpower business would ever get done. In truth, episodes like the Daniloff affair were not simply bumps in the road to summits; they were the pavement itself.

STRANGE INTERLUDE

The Daniloff affair seemed to redouble the two leaders' determination to meet face to face. Each was confident of his own ability to project an appealing but also commanding and persuasive personality. The two shared the belief that, as individuals, they could and should exert direct control over the relationship between their countries, rather than leave it to the giant bureaucracies over which they presided. The incident served as a reminder to both men of how relatively minor events can spin out of their control.

In a series of communications with the White House before Daniloff was allowed to leave the U.S.S.R., Gorbachev expressed anger over the uproar in the United States that the journalist's detention had provoked, but also frustration and impatience that the U.S.-Soviet relationship should so often seem to defy deliberate, coherent management from the top. In a letter that Shevardnadze delivered to Reagan on September 19, Gorbachev wrote of the need for the two leaders to involve themselves personally, so as to impart an "impulse" to the stalled diplomatic process. He proposed the Reykjavik meeting as a way of accelerating preparations for a Washington summit.

Reagan, according to his aides, was immediately inclined to accept. He was attracted to the symbolism of meeting the other leader in a city halfway between their two capitals. He was encouraged by Donald Regan, who felt that Reagan had proved in Geneva the year before that he could deftly handle his Soviet counterpart. Some of Regan's associates said that he also had his eye on the calendar: a mid-October meeting in Reykjavik would come a few weeks before the national elections of November 4, in which the President's party would be fighting, in vain as it turned out, to keep control of the Senate. The meeting would remind the electorate that the Republican flag was still firmly planted on diplomatic high ground.

Gorbachev's proposal was kept secret until Daniloff was safely out of the Soviet Union. Then the President stunned the world by announcing that he would go to Iceland ten days later.

The Soviets had led the Americans to expect that INF would be the focal point of the meeting. Since the Geneva summit the year before, the Soviets had been hinting, and occasionally flatly stating, that Gorbachev was prepared to sign a separate INF agreement, unlinked from other arms-control issues. But when Reagan arrived for his first session with Gorbachev in Reykjavik, he found that INF was neither the main item on the agenda nor was it detached from the other, more difficult, strategic issues. Gorbachev had brought with him a whole briefcase full of papers outlining nothing less than a comprehensive arms-control agreement dealing with INF, START, and SDI, as well as other issues such as nuclear weapons testing. In the words of one of the President's aides, the Soviet leader was "going for the big casino."

From the beginning it was clear to Reagan that while Gorbachev had come prepared to make some unexpectedly forthcoming concessions, they might all be contingent on some sort of reciprocal American flexibility in SDI, although exactly what that flexibility would have to involve was not at first apparent. Emerging from his first session with Gorbachev to meet with his American advisers, Reagan said, "He's brought a whole lot of proposals, but I'm afraid he's going after SDI."

Gorbachev was proposing a version of the grand compromise. Those who pondered the possibilities for such a compromise had never been certain about how far the Soviets would go in reducing their most threatening offensive weapon in order to obtain restraints on American defenses.

In Reykjavik, Gorbachev and his colleagues moved toward answering that question, although the answer that emerged was neither conclusive, precise, nor binding. The exact terms of the tentative accord reached during the weekend were the subject of considerable confusion. There were subsequent disagreements about exactly what had been decided, what conditions had been attached, and what timetable had been stipulated. Some reductions were slated to take place over five years, others over the course of ten. Some of the provisions for the second phase seemed more like utopian reveries or pure propaganda than real arms control. In the week that followed, senior Administration officials launched an intense public relations campaign to reverse the impression that Reykjavik had ended in failure. They engaged in a surreal debate with the Soviets, and sometimes with each other, over whether by 1996 the world was to be free of all nuclear weapons, as the Soviets contended, or only of all ballistic missiles. Neither the President nor Donald Regan was at first quite clear on that point.

During a climactic Sunday session in Reykjavik, Reagan proposed the elimination of ballistic missiles within ten years. This would have deprived the Soviet Union of its most formidable weapons while leaving the United States with an advantage in nuclear-armed bombers and cruise missiles. Gorbachev countered with a variation of a proposal he had been making since January for the elimination of all nuclear weapons, which would have left the Soviet Union with numerical advantages in conventional forces. Reagan replied, "That suits me fine."

The President subsequently maintained that he had not intended to endorse Gorbachev's call for total nuclear disarmament within ten years; rather, Reagan explained, he had merely meant to reiterate his long-standing hope that a nuclear-free world would be achieved some day.

In the week after Reykjavik, the Administration adopted a unified public stance: it was committed to the goal of eliminating all ballistic missiles within ten years. However, that objective, too, proved controversial. The Joint Chiefs of Staff were upset that they had not been given a chance to study the military implications of what would be a drastic change in the basis for deterrence. Military and congressional leaders argued that a ten-year timetable for the abolition of ballistic missiles would undercut support for the new generation of American ballistic missiles—the MX, the Midgetman and the Trident II or D-5 submarine-launched missile. By promoting the elimination of ballistic missiles within ten years, the Administration was unintentionally undermining its own much-vaunted "strategic modernization" program.

Experts on both sides of the Atlantic reminded the Administration that ballistic missiles were crucial to the credibility of the American nuclear umbrella over Western Europe; the doctrine of extended deterrence depended on the American capacity to retaliate quickly and effectively with a nuclear strike if the Soviet Union ever attacked NATO; and ballistic missiles were the principal means of carrying out that retaliation.*

During their long and tiring sessions in Iceland, Reagan and Gorbachev had apparently been caught up in a make-or-break atmosphere. At the end they had engaged in a bout of feverish one-upmanship, with each trying to outdo the other in demonstrating his devotion to the dream of a nuclear-free world. Each had reverted to his grandiose disarmament appeals of earlier in the year. That part of the documen-

*Senator Sam Nunn, an authority on defense issues, contended that without nuclear weapons the West would find itself at a disadvantage in facing the superior non-nuclear forces of the Eastern bloc and said that he was "relieved that the superpowers did not reach an agreement along these lines." Former Secretary of Defense James Schlesinger made the same point in an essay in *Time* Magazine on October 27, 1986, entitled "The Dangers of a Nuclear-Free World," in which he also asserted that abolishing nuclear weapons forever was simply not possible because the understanding of how to make them would always remain.

tary record of the weekend appeared destined to recede into the footnotes of history.

However, the terms that had been envisioned for the first five-year period were more specific, more modest, and more in line with agreements that the two sides had signed and observed in the past. The stated goal of a 50-percent across-the-board reduction in strategic weapons might not be reached in the course of the detailed negotiations that would be necessary to turn the terms into a treaty. But an accord along the lines of the Reykjavik agreement would almost certainly compel the Soviets to retire a significant portion of their large ICBMs, which have been the principal cause of American concerns about a "window of vulnerability," the driving obsession of the American strategic debate for nearly two decades. At Reykjavik, Gorbachev also agreed to provisions that would induce both sides to rely more on bombers, cruise missiles and small, single-warhead mobile ICBMs—weapons that are better suited to retaliation and therefore less likely to pose the threat of a first strike.

While the Americans wanted reductions of offensive forces, the chief Soviet goal was restraints on defensive systems — specifically the American SDI. The Soviets had earlier proposed an extension of the ABM Treaty for "up to" fifteen years, and in a letter to Gorbachev in July 1986 Reagan had proposed continuing the treaty for seven and a half years. The question of duration was obviously amenable to compromise: the two could split the difference and arrive at a figure of ten years. So they did at Reykjavik. But that did not resolve the difficult question of what the ABM Treaty actually permitted in the way of research, development and testing of high-technology space-based defensive systems. It was over that issue that the Reykjavik meeting collapsed.

Early in the weekend, Gorbachev indicated that he was interested in "strengthening" the treaty. However, not until the final unscheduled session on Sunday afternoon did he make clear that by this he meant that research must be confined to the "laboratory." Reagan balked at that formulation. As he told Gorbachev, and said repeatedly afterward, he considered this definition of permissible research an attempt to "kill" SDI. When Gorbachev would not budge, the President gathered up his papers and the meeting ended on a note of failure and recrimination.

It was perhaps the most bizarre moment in what was already a peculiar event: the President had not been prepared to deal conclusively or in detail with the vital and immensely complicated question of the future relationship between SDI and the ABM treaty; he had little opportunity to take counsel from his own advisers, not to mention from technical experts and European and congressional leaders, on a subject that had implications spanning both oceans and stretching far into the future. Yet he not only made a critical decision on the spot, he publicized it in a way that froze both leaderships into contrary positions. Why did he not simply say to Gorbachev, in effect, "This is very interesting, a lot is on the table. We'll have to study it carefully and get back to you."?

That question was not answered in the immediate post-Reykjavik flurry of official American explanation and justification. One conjecture was that Reagan felt under some pressure from the right. If he had seemed even to entertain Gorbachev's proposal, he would have been vulnerable to charges of doing at Reykjavik what he had avoided doing at Geneva the year before: compromising on SDI. Conservative congressmen and columnists had warned him not to before the meeting; they congratulated him afterward for not doing so. Even more important to the President was his deep commitment to the dream of a space shield that would protect the American people from nuclear attack. He sensed that the Soviet leader was trying to get him to give up that dream; he responded by walking away.

From the Soviet point of view, Reagan's position meant that the United States was not willing to pay any appreciable price in defensive restraints to get offensive reductions—at least not yet. Reagan's agreement to delay SDI deployment for ten years and adhere to the ABM treaty depended on the complete elimination of all ballistic missiles within that same ten-year period, something that virtually nobody outside the room in Hofdi House, where the two leaders met, considered even remotely feasible. In any event, the delay hardly represented a concession because SDI would not be ready for full deployment for ten years anyway.

Moreover, after the meeting, Administration spokesmen reiterated the permissive interpretation of the ABM treaty that Richard Perle had been pressing since 1985. In Reykjavik and back in Washington, Shultz asserted that the treaty gave the United States the right not just to conduct research, but also to develop and test an SDI system and its components. So when the ten-year moratorium ended, the United States might have a defensive system of some kind ready to put in place. Faced with that prospect, the

Soviets would have no incentive to reduce their offensive forces. Quite the contrary, they would have every reason to *increase* their arsenal of offensive weapons; for in order to deter the United States, the Soviets believe, they must be able to penetrate and overwhelm whatever defenses the United States eventually deploys. Thus, Reagan's position on the defensive half of the grand compromise at Reykjavik came down to a refusal to accept any of the restraints on SDI that the Soviets sought.

In his attempt to restrict the program to "laboratory" research, Gorbachev seemed to be insisting on a new, more restrictive interpretation of the ABM treaty, just as Reagan and Shultz were advancing a more permissive one. Each side had room to maneuver. Reagan's principal concern seemed to be protecting SDI from Soviet efforts to "kill" it. Even many who were skeptical of his vision of the program as a way to defend American cities from Soviet nuclear attack believed that the United States needed to conduct a research program to hedge against the possibility that the Soviets, who also had a research effort underway, would make a breakthrough of their own in that area.

The research program that even many skeptics supported, however, might well go forward even under the traditional interpretation of the treaty. According to Gerard Smith, who was its chief American negotiator, "There could be testing, outside the laboratory, of some new technologies and devices, as long as they were not components of a deployable system. Defining components may be a key element in the ongoing negotiation, but in the gray area between the Soviets' current 'laboratory' definition of permissible research and the Administration's claim that anything goes, there should be a way of accommodating Gorbachev's fear and Reagan's dream."

If Smith was right, the compromise that the two leaders had failed to reach at Reykjavik might yet be struck. Both leaders promised to persist in seeking one. At his press conference immediately after the meeting, Gorbachev said, "The road we have traveled toward these major agreements—major accords on the reduction of nuclear arms—gives us substantial experience, gives us substantial gains here in Reykjavik." In a televised address from Moscow two days later he said, "Probably the American leadership will need a certain amount of time. We are realists and we understand quite clearly that the issues, which for many years and even decades had not found their solution, can probably not be dealt with in one go." A week after that speech he delivered another one, in which he complained that the American side was giving a distorted version of the events in Iceland. But he reaffirmed that "we are not removing these proposals; they still stand. Everything that has been said by way of their substantiation and development remains as before. "The Rekjavik meeting," he added, "greatly facilitated, probably for the first time in many decades, our search for disarmament." These statements were a far cry from Andropov's September 1983 dismissal of any hope of further dealing with Washington.

Reagan, too, looked to further negotiation. "I'm still optimistic that a way will be found," he said in a televised speech of his own after Reykjavik. "The door is open and the opportunity to begin eliminating the nuclear threat is within reach. . . . Our ideas are out there on the table. They won't go away. We're ready to pick up where we left off. Our negotiators are heading back to Geneva, and we're prepared to go forward whenever and wherever the Soviets are ready." Within three weeks, Shultz and Shevardnadze met again, this time in Vienna, to try to pick up the pieces. That meeting failed to break the impasse over SDI, and, in Shevardnadze's words, "left a bitter taste." American officials in Vienna had the impression that the Soviets might be stalling for time to reassess the American political situation in the wake of the Democratic Party's regaining control of the Senate, two days before the meeting. Nonetheless, both Shultz and Shevardnadze called for patience and reiterated their determination to press forward on future negotiations.

Almost immediately after they ended in disappointment, therefore, the Reykjavik and Vienna meetings were already beginning to appear as another stage, a difficult and discouraging stage perhaps, but far from the last one, in the ongoing effort to regulate the military competition between the superpowers.

UPPER AND LOWER LIMITS

With the Reykjavik meeting, Reagan and Gorbachev were two-thirds of the way to matching the trio of summits that Nixon and Brezhnev had held during the heyday of détente. Relations between the United States and the Soviet Union were not, however, returning to the conditions of the early 1970s. The political arrangements of that particular period had sunk into the past, weighted down with controversies and recriminations. The Reagan-Gorbachev relationship, however it turned out, would be different. Furthermore, however the bargaining on arms control ended, the interaction of these two leaders, including the roller-coaster course of relations in 1986, demonstrated some enduring principles of the Soviet-American relationship itself. Those principles essentially concerned limits—on what the superpowers could do both to each other and with each other.

One was the limit to how far Soviet-American relations could deteriorate. Particularly during his first term, Reagan was the most anti-Soviet President in thirty years, perhaps ever. He had aimed not at solidifying the status quo in East-West relations but at overturning it. His rhetoric toward Moscow had been harsh. The Soviet leaders had responded with even harsher language of their own. Each side had tried briefly to impose a diplomatic boycott on the other. Yet at no time, even when relations were at their worst—even after the Korean airliner episode and the Soviet walkout from the Geneva talks in 1983—had there been a serious danger of war. Moreover, none of the agreements that had been reached in more cordial times came unstuck. The European settlement that the détente of the early 1970s had produced never even came under critical scrutiny. While the SALT agreements were the objects of a good deal of such scrutiny, they remained in force, at least until late 1986. And in 1985, the two leaders found themselves agreeing to meet regularly. The business they had with each other was too compelling to ignore.

The first half of the 1980s, and the policies that both sides pursued in that period, also showed that neither was likely to gain a decisive advantage over the other. By agreeing in principle to meet on a regular basis and to seek diplomatic accommodation on some of the issues that divided them, the two leaders were implicitly acknowledging the limits of their ability to get their way unilaterally. For both men, this was a lesson that took some time to learn.

In his June 1982 address to the British Parliament, Reagan had called the Soviet Union "inherently unstable" and said that it was facing a "great revolutionary crisis." He had implied that the United States should exploit that instability and aggravate that crisis. By the time he first met with Gorbachev in November 1985, he had ceased to make such claims. He had even signed a presidential directive that concluded that the United States had at best only a very modest ability to influence internal Soviet policy and should focus instead on influencing its external policy.

One way to influence the foreign policy of the Soviet Union was to discourage Soviet expansionism by supporting anti-Soviet insurgencies in the Third World. The Reagan Doctrine, which committed the United States to such support, was still very much in force at the time of Reykjavik. But that hallmark policy of the Administration was encountering difficulties at home. On the issue of Nicaragua, the White House was under public and congressional pressure to couple the military and paramilitary aid for the contras with genuine support for the diplomatic effort to achieve a negotiated settlement, known as the Contadora process.

Meanwhile, there were signs that the Soviets, too, had begun to understand the limits of unilateralism in the competition in nuclear weapons. Marshal

Ogarkov, the former Chief of the Soviet General Staff, spoke of the fruitlessness of the arms race and said that nuclear superiority was a mirage. Soviet specialists on strategic affairs not only called for a "new way of thinking" about the problems of stability—some of them sometimes also tentatively attempted to think and write in new ways.*

Among the most interesting statements that Gorbachev made during his first eighteen months in power concerned what he and other Soviet spokesmen referred to as "common security." At the end of the Geneva summit he expressed his "profound conviction that less security for the United States of America compared to the Soviet Union would not be in our interests, since it could lead to mistrust and produce instability." He elaborated on this theme in his address to the Twenty-seventh Party Congress three months later: "The character of present-day weapons leaves a country no hope of safeguarding itself solely with military and technical means. The task of ensuring security is increasingly seen as a political problem, and can be resolved only by political means . . . Security can only be mutual . . . It is vital that all should feel equally secure, for fears and anxieties of the nuclear age generate unpredictability in politics and concrete actions."

*Two interesting examples: *Novoye myshleniye v yaderny vek* (New Thinking in the Nuclear Age), by Anatoli Gromyko, the son of the former Foreign Minister, and Vladimir Lomeiko, the former spokesman for the Foreign Ministry; and *Voyenno-strategichesky paritet i politika SSHA* (Military-Strategic Parity and the Policy of the USA), by Aleksei Arbatov, a leading Soviet analyst and the son of the U.S.S.R.'s best known "Americanist," Georgi Arbatov, the director of the Institute for the Study of the USA and Canada.

Gorbachev's reassuring words may simply have been part of another Soviet campaign to lull and divide the West. But they may also have reflected the beginning of a welcome if belated Soviet recognition that the Leninist principle that politics is always a matter of *kto-kogo*—who will prevail over whom—was simply not operative, or for that matter even acceptable, in the strategic nuclear relationship. Gorbachev's words may have bespoken a Soviet conclusion similar to the one strategists in the West had long since reached: However fiercely they may compete elsewhere, in conducting the nuclear arms race the superpowers best serve their own interests by maintaining an equilibrium and jointly fostering the goal of strategic stability. Even though many details remained to be clarified and negotiated, the terms to which the Soviets agreed in Reykjavik suggested that they might indeed be prepared eventually to accommodate some American concerns and cooperate to achieve a more stable nuclear balance.

SDI had undoubtedly played an important part in forcing Gorbachev, Ogarkov and others to rethink what common security meant in the strategic nuclear competition. It had forced them to face up to some of the more dangerous consequences of their excessive accumulation of land-based ballistic missile warheads. If they pressed for advantages in the familiar area of offensive weapons, they might find themselves plunging into the unfamiliar and treacherous terrain of high-technology strategic defense. To make matters worse, the Americans would have arrived there first, and would feel much more at home.

Reagan, too, came up against obstacles to altering the nuclear relationship between the superpowers.

As he made clearer than ever at Reykjavik, SDI was his bid to change the rules, indeed to change the game itself. But by then, for all his devotion to SDI and for all the disagreements about how the ABM treaty should be interpreted, he found himself having to offer repeated assurances that the program could proceed under the terms of the treaty. SDI therefore seemed likely to flourish only to the extent that it was compatible with deterrence and arms control. Reykjavik was bound to increase the pressure to use it as a bargaining chip to get reductions in offensive weapons. That rationale was a far cry from the President's original vision, proclaimed in March 1983, of an impregnable Astrodome over the United States that would render nuclear weapons "impotent and obsolete."

Indeed, while Reagan's conduct at Reykjavik demonstrated he still believed in that vision, few officials outside the Oval Office of the White House shared his hope. Virtually his entire government either had abandoned the idea of a comprehensive defense that would make traditional deterrence unnecessary, or had never subscribed to the idea in the first place. Richard Perle's preference for defending missiles instead of cities and Paul Nitze's stringent criteria for a system of space-based defenses could each be seen as an implicit admission of the failure of the Reagan vision of abolishing the threat of nuclear war and escaping the dilemma of deterrence. Perle and Nitze were at odds over how to deal with the asymmetry in land-based missiles, the question that the strategic community had been debating for over fifteen years. But that was a disagreement about how to improve the existing condition of mutual assured destruction, not whether to do away with it, as the President dreamed. While Reagan serenely maintained his vision of a world free of nuclear weapons, everybody else—Perle and Nitze, Gorbachev and Ogarkov—was arguing about how to preserve the status quo.

If the Reagan-Gorbachev relationship demonstrates the limits to both what the superpowers can do to thwart each other and how far their relations can deteriorate, it also illustrates the upper limits on improvement in their relations. The potential accord that was glimpsed at Reykjavik could go beyond the limitations on offensive weapons established by the SALT II treaty. But the grand compromise, if it ever comes about, will scarcely represent a whole new approach to strategic arms control. Quite the contrary, it would reaffirm not just SALT II but SALT I by linking limits on strategic defense with restrictions on strategic offense.

Thus, even as they broke with some of the procedures that their predecessors had followed, Reagan and Gorbachev were moving in the direction of restoring a measure of continuity with the past. Moreover, just as he had learned to live and work with Gorbachev, Reagan had learned to live with the old, familiar problems of asymmetries in force structures, theoretical vulnerabilities and the moral as well as practical difficulties of deterrence.

If the worst that is likely to happen between the superpowers is not all that bad, the best is not all that good. A genuine transformation in Soviet-American relations will depend not on grandiose but impractical visions of a world free of nuclear weapons or even on concrete arms-control compromises. Rather, it will depend on internal changes in the Soviet Union. As long as Moscow defines its security in a way that makes many of its own citizens and much of the rest of the world feel highly insecure, the challenge to the United States will remain, whether the Strategic Rocket Forces deploy 308 SS-18 missiles or 150 or none at all.

Whether Gorbachev will preside over fundamental changes in the Soviet system is a question that probably not even he can answer less than two years into what he doubtless hopes will be a long tenure in office. By the fall of 1986, he had become proficient at delivering bold exhortations to the people and the ruling class of the Soviet Union. There had to be a massive *perestroika*, he said, an overhaul or restructuring of the economic and social order. He quoted Lenin as defining a revolutionary situation as one in which the people down below are unwilling, and the people on top are unable, to live in the old way. The clear implication was that the Soviet Union found itself in just such a situation. Gorbachev seemed to be offering himself as the leader of a revolution within the revolution. He also dropped broad hints that he was encountering resistance not only from the *narod* (the people), but from the *apparat* of the Party, the *nomenklatura* (the privileged class) of the state and probably from within the Politburo itself.

What exactly Gorbachev will do under the banner of *perestroika* is not clear, but it will surely involve more than discouraging the consumption of alcohol and replacing seventy-year-old apparatchiks with fifty-year-old technocrats, although both measures are undoubtedly steps in what he considers the right direction. The larger question is whether he is willing—and if willing, able—to change the emphasis of the Soviet system from coercion and centralized control to individual initiative and responsibility. Such a Soviet Union could be expected to treat its "fraternal" neighbors of Eastern Europe less like a fortified buffer zone and more like a commonwealth. Its relations toward other foreign countries would similarly become more benign. Only if that turns out to be the direction in which he takes the Soviet Union will a truly fundamental change in Soviet-American relations be in prospect.

That prospect is remote at best. No matter how Gorbachev comes to define *perestroika* in practice and no matter how he modifies the official definition of security, the Soviet Union will resist pressure for change, whether it comes from without or within, from the top or the bottom. The fundamental conditions of Soviet-American relations are therefore likely to persist. This, in turn, means that the ritual of Soviet-American summitry is likely to have a long run, and for all the reasons that led Reagan and Gorbachev to engage in that ritual themselves, both in the fairly traditional summit at Geneva in November 1985 and in the strange interlude at Reykjavik a year later.

Gorbachev's successor, or his successor's successor, will probably some day meet at a guesthouse in Geneva or Camp David or a dacha outside Moscow with an American President now in a state legislature, or law school, or high school. The two will bring to that meeting Wilson's and Lenin's legacy of global ideological rivalry, Roosevelt's and Stalin's heritage of a divided Europe, Kennedy's and Khrushchev's mutual recognition of the perils of confrontation, and Nixon's and Brezhnev's preliminary, flawed, but surprisingly durable attempt to regulate the arms race. Whoever they are, and whatever changes have occurred in the meantime, the American and Soviet leaders of the next century will be wrestling with the same great issue—how to manage their rivalry so as to avoid nuclear catastrophe—that has engaged the energies, in the latter half of the 1980s, of Ronald Reagan and Mikhail Gorbachev.

ABOUT THE AUTHORS

Michael Mandelbaum is a Senior Fellow and Director of the Project on East-West Relations at the Council on Foreign Relations. He is the author of *The Nuclear Question: The United States and Nuclear Weapons, 1946–1976* (1979), *The Nuclear Revolution: International Politics Before and After Hiroshima* (1981) and *The Nuclear Future* (1983).

Strobe Talbott is the Washington Bureau Chief of *Time* Magazine. He is the translator and editor of *Khrushchev Remembers* (1970) and *Khrushchev Remembers: The Last Testament* (1974) and the author of *Endgame: The Inside Story of SALT II* (1979), *The Russians and Reagan* (1984), and *Deadly Gambits: The Reagan Administration and the Stalemate in Arms Control* (1984).